Essential Weekend Recipes

Make Saturdays and Sundays Fun with Unique and Easy Meals

By
BookSumo Press
All rights reserved

Published by
http://www.booksumo.com

Table of Contents

Italian Spring Pasta Salad 7

Fruity Salmon Macaroni Salad with Yogurt Dressing 8

Balsamic Romaine Shells Salad 9

Fruity Curry Shells Salad 10

Garbanzo Bows Pasta 11

Broccoli Romano Ravioli Salad 12

Cocktail Shrimp Macaroni Salad 13

Tri-colored Greek Style Pasta Salad 14

Hot Pasta Spirals Salad 15

Rotini Crabmeat Salad 16

Greek Rotini Salad with Lemon Dressing 17

Cheesy Italian Pizza Burger 18

Balsamic Mayo Burgers 19

Italian Balsamic Mushroom Burger 20

Sea Lentils Burgers 21

Birdie Burgers 22

Tamari Burger Casserole 23

Crunchy and Juicy Noodles Burgers 24

Baby Cheddar Burger 26

Rolled Kidney Bean Burgers 27

Jalapeno Fritos Burger 28

White Steak Burgers 29

Soupy Onion Burger 30

Thai Bell Bean Burgers 31

Vidalia Turkey Burgers 32

Saucy Hot Winter Soup 34

Addictive Carrot Juice Soup 35

Tex Mex Turkey Soup 36

Hot and Sweet Soup 37

Marjoram Liver Soup 38

Lime Beef Soup 39

Chunky Messy Garden Soup 40

Black Pea Sirloin Soup 41

Consommé Jungle Soup 42

Italian Worcestershire Soup 43

Bell Green Beef Soup 44

Tabasco Soup 45

Asian Anise Soup 46

Classic French Soup 47

Quinoa Festival 48

Chicken, Cucumbers, & Parsley Couscous 49

Lime and Chicken Couscous 50

Peppers, Corn, and Black Beans Couscous 51

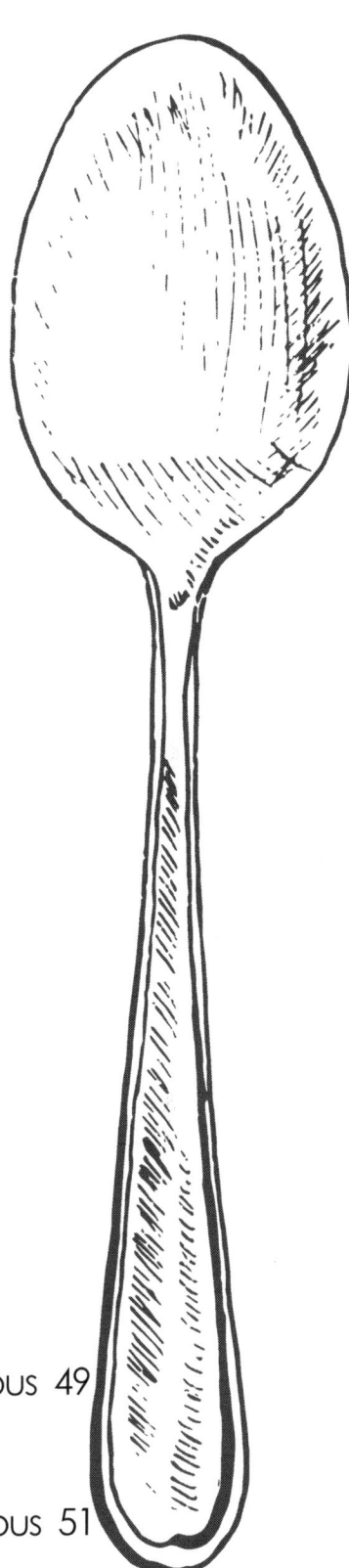

Creamy Parsley, Chickpeas, and Almonds Couscous 52

Veggie Turkey Couscous Bits Couscous 53

Squash and Garbanzos Couscous 54

Cherry Tomatoes, Onions, and Basil Couscous 55

Chipotle Quinoa 56

Mangos, and Salsa Couscous 57

Quinoa Summer Salad 58

Moroccan Salmon Cake Couscous 59

Rustic Quinoa 60

Pecans, Parmesan, and Pesto Couscous 61

Lunchtime Quinoa 62

Honey Rutabaga Couscous 63

Quinoa Classico 64

Mexican Pineapple and Beans Couscous 65

Quinoa Forever 66

Green Beans and Black Beans Couscous 67

Deluxe Fish Tacos 68

Lime Beef Tacos 69

Vegetarian Swiss Tacos 70

Avocado Tacos Supreme 71

Coleslaw Tacos 72

Arizona Tacos 73

Shrimp Tacos 74

Teriyaki Tacos 75

Cilantro BBQ Corn 76

Tostadas 77

Thursday's Quesadilla's 78

Aztec Corn Bread 79

Chicago Hot Dogs 80

Simple Spring Lunch Hot Dogs 81

Saucy Spanish Mussels 82

Mussels Martinique 83

Mussels Toscano 84

Creamy Dijon Mussels 85

Topped Mussel Platter 86

Country Style Mussels with Leeks 87

Mussels Marrakesh 88

Florida Mussel Soup 89

Creamy City Mussels 90

Cajun Style Tilapia I 91

Easy Veggie Baked Tilapia 92

Raspberries and Dijon Tilapia 93

Teriyaki Chicken Stir Fry with Noodles 94

Tangerine Chicken Stir Fry 95

Basmati Chicken Stir Fry Spears 97

Grilled Chicken Stir Fry Linguine 98

Beachy Chicken Stir Fry 99

Fried Teriyaki Chicken Rice 100

American Parsley Chicken Stir Fry 101

Spicy Chicken Noodles Stir Fry 102

Spicy Chestnut Chicken Stir Fry 103

Carrot, Cabbage, and Chicken Skillet 104

Sweet and Salty Chicken Stir Fry 105

Chili Fried Chicken Breast Bites 106

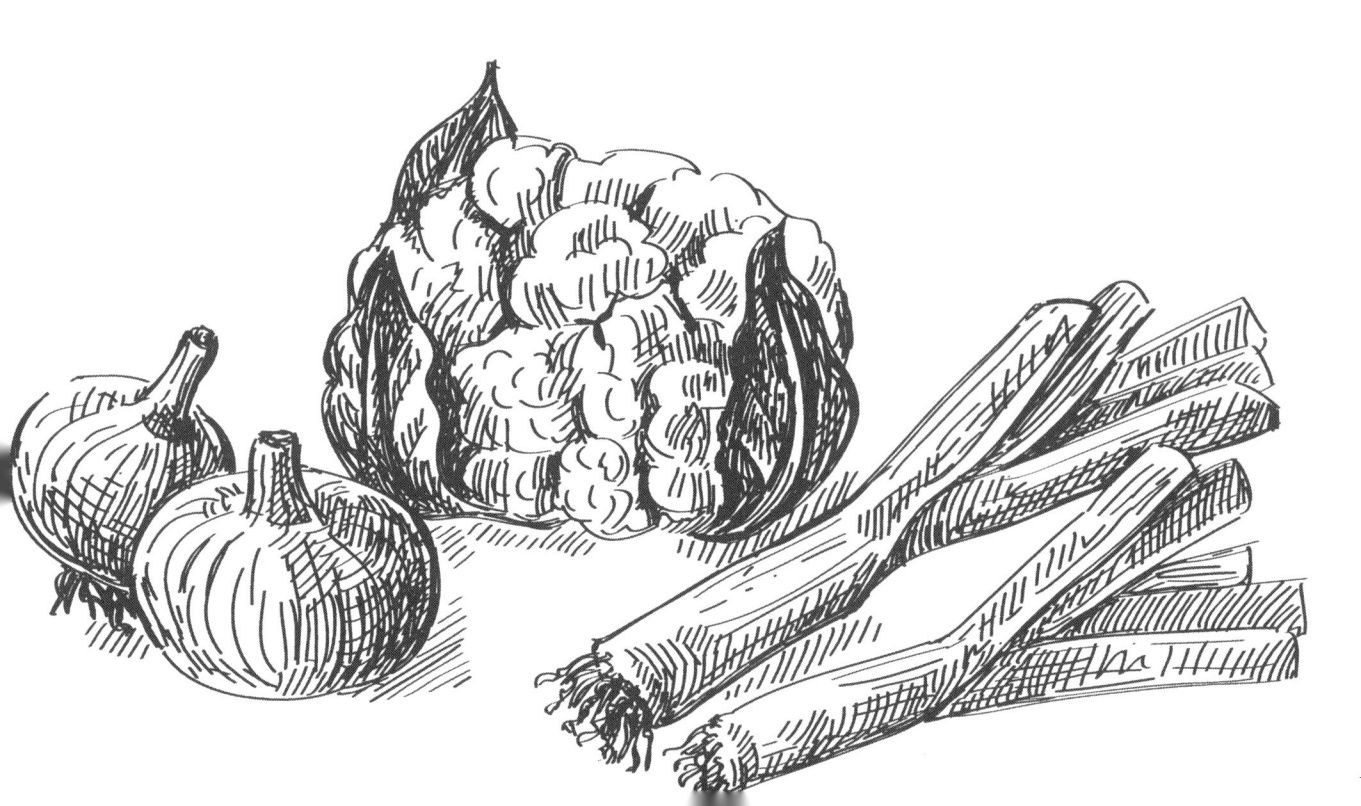

Italian Spring Pasta Salad

🥣 Prep Time: 20 mins
🕒 Total Time: 20 mins

Servings per Recipe: 8
Calories	233 kcal
Fat	12.2 g
Carbohydrates	26.2g
Protein	6.6 g
Cholesterol	9 mg
Sodium	598 mg

Ingredients

- 8 oz rotelle or spiral pasta, cooked and drained
- 2 1/2 C. assorted cut-up vegetables (broccoli, carrots, tomatoes, bell peppers, cauliflower, onions and mushrooms)
- 1/2 C. cubed Cheddar or mozzarella cheese
- 1/3 C. sliced pitted ripe olives (optional)
- 1 C. Wish-Bone(R) Italian Dressing

Directions

1. Get a large mixing bowl: Combine in it the pasta with veggies, cheddar cheese and olives. Toss them well.
2. Drizzle the dressing on top. Adjust the seasoning of the salad and serve it.
3. Enjoy.

FRUITY SALMON
Macaroni Salad with Yogurt Dressing

Prep Time: 10 mins
Total Time: 40 mins

Servings per Recipe: 8
Calories   222 kcal
Fat   12.3 g
Carbohydrates   17.6 g
Protein   11 g
Cholesterol   18 mg
Sodium   208 mg

Ingredients

1 C. dry pasta, such as macaroni or small shells
8 oz cooked, skinned salmon
1/2 C. minced red or yellow onion
1 C. diced celery
1 medium red apple, diced
1/2 C. chopped walnuts or dry-roasted, unsalted peanuts
Dressing:
1 (6 oz) container fat-free yogurt

2 tbsp olive oil
1 tbsp curry powder
2 tsp fresh lemon juice
2 cloves garlic, crushed
1 tsp Dijon mustard
1/2 tsp salt (or to taste)
Freshly ground black pepper, to taste

Directions

1. Cook the pasta according to the directions on the package.
2. Get a small mixing bowl: Combine in it the dressing ingredients. Mix them well.
3. Get a large mixing bowl: Combine in it the salad ingredients. Add the dressing and stir them well.
4. Adjust the seasoning of the salad. Place it in the fridge until ready to serve.
5. Enjoy.

Balsamic Romaine Shells Salad

Prep Time: 20 mins
Total Time: 30 mins

Servings per Recipe: 9
Calories	312 kcal
Fat	14.7 g
Carbohydrates	30.7g
Protein	14.3 g
Cholesterol	32 mg
Sodium	819 mg

Ingredients

- 18 jumbo pasta shells
- 1/2 lb thinly sliced beef salami
- 4 C. chopped romaine lettuce
- 1 C. chopped roma tomatoes
- 3/4 C. seeded and chopped cucumber
- 3/4 C. chopped red onion
- 1/2 C. balsamic vinaigrette salad dressing
- 1 C. shredded Parmesan cheese

Directions

1. Cook the pasta according to the directions on the package.
2. Get a large mixing bowl: Toss in it the pasta with salami, romaine lettuce, roma tomatoes, cucumber, and red onion. Drizzle the balsamic vinegar on top.
3. Mix them well. Spoon the mix into the pasta shells to stuff them with it. Place the pasta shells on a serving shallow bowl. Sprinkle the cheese on top then serve it.
4. Enjoy.

FRUITY CURRY
Shells Salad

Prep Time: 25 mins
Total Time: 1 hr 40 mins

Servings per Recipe: 8
Calories	374 kcal
Fat	32.2 g
Carbohydrates	17.6 g
Protein	5.1 g
Cholesterol	10 mg
Sodium	515 mg

Ingredients

- 8 slices turkey bacon
- 1/2 C. uncooked shell pasta
- 2 tbsp white vinegar
- 1/4 C. white sugar
- 1 1/2 tbsp dried basil
- 1 tbsp dried thyme
- 4 cloves garlic, peeled
- 1 tsp salt
- 1 tsp curry powder
- 1/2 tsp ground black pepper
- 1 C. canola oil
- 4 peaches, peeled and cut into chunks
- 1/2 C. chopped fresh parsley
- 1/2 C. sliced celery
- 1/2 C. chopped red bell pepper
- 6 green onions, chopped

Directions

1. Place a large pan over medium heat. Cook in it the bacon for 12 min until it becomes crisp.
2. Remove it from the grease and place it aside to drain and lose heat. Press the bacon until it becomes crumbled and place it aside.
3. Cook the pasta according to the directions on the package.
4. Get a food processor: Combine in it the vinegar, sugar, basil, thyme, garlic, salt, curry powder, and black pepper. Process them until they become smooth.
5. Add to it the oil in a steady stream while blending all the time until the dressing becomes creamy.
6. Get a large mixing bowl: Toss in it the pasta with bacon, dressing, peaches, parsley, celery, red bell pepper, and green onions.
7. Adjust the seasoning of the salad. Place the salad in the fridge for 1 h 10 min then serve it.
8. Enjoy.

Garbanzo Bows Pasta

Prep Time: 18 mins
Total Time: 30 mins

Servings per Recipe: 10
Calories   207 kcal
Fat   14.5 g
Carbohydrates   15.5g
Protein   4.5 g
Cholesterol   11 mg
Sodium   414 mg

Ingredients

- 2 1/2 C. bow tie (farfalle) pasta
- 1 C. Greek salad dressing
- 2 1/2 tbsp mayonnaise
- 4 radishes, finely chopped
- 1/2 cucumber, peeled and chopped
- 1 (15 oz) can garbanzo beans, drained
- 3/4 C. crumbled feta cheese

Directions

1. Cook the pasta according to the directions on the package.
2. Get a large mixing bowl: Combine in it the Greek dressing and mayonnaise. Mix them well. Stir in the pasta.
3. Add the radishes, cucumber, garbanzo beans, and crumbled feta cheese and stir them gently. Adjust the seasoning of the salad then serve it.
4. Enjoy.

BROCCOLI ROMANO
Ravioli Salad

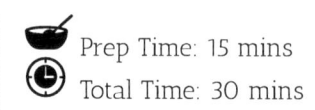

⏲ Prep Time: 15 mins
🕐 Total Time: 30 mins

Servings per Recipe: 4
Calories	653 kcal
Fat	31.7 g
Carbohydrates	66.9g
Protein	28 g
Cholesterol	63 mg
Sodium	902 mg

Ingredients

2 (9 oz) packages BUITONI(R) Refrigerated Light Four Cheese Ravioli, prepared according to package directions, chilled
1/4 C. extra virgin olive oil
4 large cloves garlic, finely chopped
1/4 C. balsamic vinegar
2 medium tomatoes, chopped
2 C. broccoli florets
1 large green bell pepper, chopped
1/2 C. pitted and halved ripe olives
1/2 C. BUITONI(R) Refrigerated Freshly Shredded Parmesan Cheese
1/4 C. BUITONI(R) Refrigerated Freshly Shredded Romano Cheese

Directions

1. Place a large saucepan over medium heat: Heat the oil in it. Add the garlic and cook it for 60 min.
2. Get a large mixing bowl: Transfer the garlic mix to it and allow it to lose heat for few minutes. Add the vinegar and mix them well.
3. Combine in the pasta, tomatoes, broccoli, bell pepper, olives, Parmesan cheese and Romano cheese. Mix them well.
4. Adjust the seasoning of the pasta. Serve it right away.
5. Enjoy.

Cocktail Shrimp Macaroni Salad

Prep Time: 20 mins
Total Time: 1 hr 30 mins

Servings per Recipe: 6
Calories	528 kcal
Fat	41 g
Carbohydrates	31.9 g
Protein	9.5 g
Cholesterol	56 mg
Sodium	920 mg

Ingredients

- 1/2 (12 oz) package elbow macaroni
- 2 stalks celery, coarsely chopped
- 1 onion, finely chopped
- 1 cucumber - peeled, seeded, and diced
- 1 tomato, diced
- 1 C. cooked small shrimp
- 1 C. Italian salad dressing
- 1 C. mayonnaise, or to taste

Directions

1. Cook the pasta according to the directions on the package.
2. Get a large mixing bowl: Combine in it the pasta with celery, onion, cucumber, tomato, shrimp, and Italian salad dressing.
3. Place the salad in the fridge for 1 h 30 min. Stir in the mayo. Adjust the seasoning of the salad then serve it right away.
4. Enjoy.

TRI-COLORED Greek Style Pasta Salad

Prep Time: 30 mins
Total Time: 5 hrs 10 mins

Servings per Recipe: 8
Calories   248 kcal
Fat   12.7 g
Carbohydrates   24.9 g
Protein   9 g
Cholesterol   9 mg
Sodium   482 mg

Ingredients

1/2 red onion, cut into bite-size pieces
4 C. ice water, or as needed
1 (8 oz) package tri-color rotini pasta
1 (5 oz) can light tuna in water, drained and flaked
2 stalks celery, cut into bite-size pieces
1/2 C. roasted red peppers, drained and chopped
1/4 C. smoked sun-dried tomatoes
1/4 C. crumbled feta cheese
1 sprig parsley, stemmed and leaves minced
4 leaves fresh basil, rolled and very thinly sliced
2 tsp capers
1 C. Greek vinaigrette salad dressing

Directions

1. Get a large bowl and fill it with ice water. Place the red onion in it and place it in the fridge for 35 min. Remove the onion from the water.
2. Cook the pasta according to the directions on the package.
3. Get a large mixing bowl: Combine in it the onion, pasta, tuna, celery, roasted red peppers, sun-dried tomatoes, feta cheese, parsley, basil, capers, and Greek dressing.
4. Stir them well. Place the salad in the fridge for 5 h to an overnight. Serve your salad with your favorite toppings.
5. Enjoy.

Hot Pasta Spirals Salad

Prep Time: 20 mins
Total Time: 2 hrs 30 mins

Servings per Recipe: 8
Calories   190 kcal
Fat   7.4 g
Carbohydrates   27.1g
Protein   4.7 g
Cholesterol   0 mg
Sodium   336 mg

Ingredients

1 (8 oz) package pasta spirals
1/4 C. diced sweet onion
1 green bell pepper, seeded and minced
1/2 fresh hot chile pepper, seeded and minced
2 tomatoes, seeded and chopped
1 cucumber, seeded and chopped
1/4 C. olive oil
1/4 C. tomato sauce
1/4 C. lime juice
3 tbsp balsamic vinegar
1 tsp garlic powder
1 tsp salt
ground black pepper to taste

Directions

1. Cook the pasta according to the directions on the package.
2. Get a small mixing bowl: Combine in it the olive oil, tomato sauce, lime juice, balsamic vinegar, garlic powder, salt, and black pepper. Mix them well to make the dressing.
3. Get a large mixing bowl: Combine in tit the pasta, sweet onion, green bell pepper, chile pepper, tomatoes, and cucumber.
4. Drizzle the dressing on top and toss the salad well. Adjust the seasoning of the salad and place it in the fridge for 2 h 30 min then serve it.
5. Enjoy.

ROTINI
Crabmeat Salad

Prep Time: 10 mins
Total Time: 30 mins

Servings per Recipe: 12
Calories   178 kcal
Fat   2 g
Carbohydrates   33.6g
Protein   6.2 g
Cholesterol   4 mg
Sodium   373 mg

Ingredients

1 (12 oz) package rotini pasta
1 (10 oz) package frozen peas, thawed
1 (8 oz) can water chestnuts, chopped
1 (8 oz) package imitation crabmeat,
coarsely chopped - or more to taste
1 C. reduced-fat mayonnaise

2 tbsp chopped fresh chives
1 tbsp chopped fresh dill

Directions

1. Cook the pasta according to the directions on the package.
2. Get a large mixing bowl: Combine in it all the ingredients. Toss them well. Adjust the seasoning of the salad then serve it.
3. Enjoy.

Greek Rotini Salad with Lemon Dressing

Prep Time: 20 mins
Total Time: 9 hrs 33 mins

Servings per Recipe: 8
Calories	453 kcal
Fat	24.9 g
Carbohydrates	50g
Protein	8.9 g
Cholesterol	8 mg
Sodium	1539 mg

Ingredients

1 (16 oz) package tri-color rotini pasta
3 1/2 tbsp lemon juice
2 1/2 tbsp canola oil
3/4 C. mayonnaise
2 1/2 tbsp seasoned salt
1 1/4 tsp flavor enhancer
2 cucumbers, seeded and diced
2 tomatoes, seeded and diced
1 (5 oz) jar sliced pimento-stuffed green olives
1 (3 oz) can chopped black olives
1/4 C. chopped green bell pepper
1/4 C. chopped green onions

Directions

1. Cook the pasta according to the directions on the package.
2. Get a small mixing bowl: Combine in it the lemon juice and canola oil. Mix them well. Add the mayonnaise, seasoned salt, and flavor enhancer then mix them again.
3. Get a large mixing bowl: Toss in it the pasta with dressing. Place it the fridge for an overnight.
4. Add the cucumbers, tomatoes, green olives, black olives, green bell pepper, and green onions to the pasta mix. Toss them well.
5. Adjust the seasoning of the salad then serve it.
6. Enjoy.

CHEESY ITALIAN
Pizza Burger

Prep Time: 15 mins
Total Time: 30 mins

Servings per Recipe: 16
Calories   322 kcal
Fat   19.1 g
Carbohydrates   18.6g
Protein   18.9 g
Cholesterol   66 mg
Sodium   953 mg

Ingredients

2 lbs ground beef
1 (12 oz.) container fully cooked luncheon meat (e.g. turkey Spam), cubed, optional
12 oz. processed cheese food, cubed
2 small onions, chopped
1 (10.75 oz.) can condensed tomato soup
1 (6 oz.) can tomato paste
1/2 tsp garlic salt
1 1/2 tsps dried oregano
8 hamburger buns split

Directions

1. Before you do anything preheat the oven to 350 F.
2. Place a large skillet on medium heat. Add the beef and cook it for 12 min. discard the fat.
3. Get a food processor: Add the luncheon meat, cheese and onion combine them until they become chopped.
4. Get a mixing bowl: Add the chopped onion mix with beef, tomato soup, tomato paste, garlic salt, and oregano. Mix them well.
5. Spoon the beef mix into the burger buns. Place them on a lined up baking sheet. Cook them in the oven for 1 min. Serve your burgers warm right away.
6. Enjoy.

Balsamic Mayo Burgers

Prep Time: 15 mins
Total Time: 2 hrs 40 mins

Servings per Recipe: 4
Calories   375 kcal
Fat   22.5 g
Carbohydrates   337.8g
Protein   7.1 g
Cholesterol   21 mg
Sodium   2459 mg

Ingredients

- 4 large Portobello mushroom caps
- 1/2 C. soy sauce
- 1/2 C. balsamic vinegar
- 4 cloves garlic, chopped, or more to taste
- 1 large red bell pepper
- 1 C. reduced-fat mayonnaise
- 1 tbsp cayenne pepper, or to taste
- 4 hamburger buns split

Directions

1. Get a zip lock bag: Add the mushroom with soy sauce, balsamic vinegar, and garlic. Shake the bag roughly to coat the ingredients. Place it aside for 2 h 30 min.
2. Before you do anything heat the grill and grease it.
3. Cook the bell pepper for 6 min on each side. Drain the mushroom caps from the marinade and cook them for 7 min on each side.
4. Transfer the bell pepper to a zip lock bag and seal it and place them aside for 5 min sweat. Peel the bell peppers and chop them.
5. Get a mixing bowl: Add the roasted bell pepper with mayo and cayenne pepper. Mix them well. Place it in the fridge until ready to serve.
6. Assemble your burgers with your favorite toppings. Serve them right away.
7. Enjoy.

ITALIAN Balsamic Mushroom Burger

Prep Time: 30 mins
Total Time: 55 mins

Servings per Recipe: 8
Calories   778 kcal
Fat   43.5 g
Carbohydrates   41.1g
Protein   53.7 g
Cholesterol   232 mg
Sodium   1386 mg

Ingredients

- 8 slices turkey bacon
- 1/2 white onion, diced
- 1 clove garlic, minced
- 1 tbsp balsamic vinegar, or to taste
- 5 fresh mushrooms, chopped
- 1/2 lb ground beef
- 1/2 C. dry bread crumbs
- 1 tsp Italian seasoning
- 1 1/2 tbsps grated Parmesan cheese
- 1 egg
- Salt and pepper to taste
- 1 malted wheat hamburger bun, split in half
- 2 slices tomato
- 2 slices Swiss cheese

Directions

1. Before you do anything preheat the oven to 375 F.
2. Place a large skillet on medium heat. Add the bacon and cook it until it becomes crunchy. Drain it and place it aside.
3. Add the garlic with onion to the bacon grease in the skillet. Cook them for 4 min on medium heat. Stir in the balsamic vinegar then cook them for 1 min.
4. Stir in the mushroom and cook them for 4 min. turn off the heat. Chop the 4 cooked bacon strips.
5. Get a mixing bowl: Add the chopped bacon, ground beef, bread crumbs, Italian seasoning, Parmesan cheese, mushroom mix and egg, salt and pepper. Combine them well.
6. Shape the mix into 2 burgers. Place the burgers on the bottom sandwich buns then top them with tomato, 2 strips of the bacon and one slice of Swiss cheese.
7. Cover the burgers with the upper buns. Serve your burgers right away.
8. Enjoy.

Sea Lentils Burgers

Prep Time: 10 mins
Total Time: 1 hr

Servings per Recipe: 3
Calories   248.8
Fat   2.4g
Cholesterol   0.0mg
Sodium   240.7mg
Carbohydrates   47.4g
Protein   110.4g

Ingredients

- 1 C. lentils (dry measure)
- 1 onion, diced
- 3 carrots, grated
- 3/4 C. whole grain flour (approx.)
- 1 pinch sea salt
- 1 tsp coriander
- 1 tsp cumin
- 1/4 tsp cayenne pepper
- 1 pinch black pepper
- 1 - 2 tsp olive oil

Directions

1. Bring a salted pot of water to a boil. Add the lentils and cook it until it is done. Drain it.
2. Get a mixing bowl: Add the carrot with onion and lentils then press them slightly with a fork to mash them a bit. Add the flour with seasoning, salt and pepper then mix them well.
3. Place a large skillet on medium heat. Add the olive oil and heat it. Shape the lentils mix into 3 burgers. Cook them in the heated skillet for 9 min on each side.
4. Assemble your burgers with your favorite toppings. Serve them right away.
5. Enjoy.

BIRDIE
Burgers

Prep Time: 5 mins
Total Time: 20 mins

Servings per Recipe: 6
Calories   479 kcal
Fat   27.2 g
Carbohydrates   25.2g
Protein   31.5 g
Cholesterol   96 mg
Sodium   467 mg

Ingredients

1 1/2 lbs lean ground beef
1 C. Birds Eye(R) Recipe Ready Chopped Onions & Garlic
6 slices Cheddar cheese
6 hamburger buns
Lettuce leaves

Directions

1. Before you do anything preheat the grill.
2. Get a mixing bowl: Add the beef and Recipe Ready Chopped Onions, Garlic, salt and pepper. Mix them well. Form them into 6 burgers.
3. Cook them in the grill for 7 min on each side. Assemble your burgers with cheddar cheese slices and lettuce leaves. Serve them right away.
4. Enjoy.

Tamari Burger Casserole

Prep Time: 40 mins
Total Time: 1 hr 40 mins

Servings per Recipe: 6
Calories   258.2
Fat   9.7g
Cholesterol   3.8mg
Sodium   907.3mg
Carbohydrates   33.1g
Protein   110.9g

Ingredients

- 2 tbsps olive oil
- 1 large yellow onion, chopped
- 1 large carrot, chopped
- 4 ounces white mushrooms, chopped
- 1 tbsp tomato paste
- 2 tbsps tamari or 2 tbsps other soy sauce
- 1 C. of basic vegetable broth
- 1 tsp minced fresh thyme
- 1 tsp minced fresh marjoram
- Salt & fresh ground pepper
- 1 tbsp cornstarch, dissolved in
- 2 tbsps water
- 3 frozen veggie burgers, thawed and crumbled
- 1/2 C. frozen green pea
- 1/4 C. ground walnuts
- 3 C. mashed potatoes (try a mix of Yukon and sweet potatoes or squash & parsnips)
- 1/4 tsp paprika

Directions

1. Before you do anything preheat the oven to 375 F. Grease a casserole dish. Place it aside.
2. Place a lire skillet on medium heat. Add 1 tbsp of olive oil. Stir in the carrot with onion. Put on the lid and cook them for 6 min. Stir in the mushroom. Cook them for 4 min.
3. Add the tomato paste, tamari, veggie stock, thyme, marjoram, cornstarch mix, salt and pepper. Simmer them for 2 min. Fold in the burgers with walnuts and peas, seasonings, salt and pepper.
4. Lay the burger mix in the casserole. Lay on it the potato then top it with paprika and the rest of the olive oil.
5. Cook the burger casserole in the oven for 34 min. serve your burger casserole right away.
6. Enjoy.

CRUNCHY and Juicy Noodles Burgers

Prep Time: 20 mins
Total Time: 1 hr

Servings per Recipe: 3
Calories   742 kcal
Fat   55.7 g
Carbohydrates   13.4g
Protein   45.9 g
Cholesterol   417 mg
Sodium   11816 mg

Ingredients

2 (3 oz.) packages instant ramen noodles, flavor packet discarded
2 large eggs
Salt and ground black pepper to taste
3/4 lb lean ground beef
1 tbsp soy sauce
1 tsp sesame oil
3 tbsps vegetable oil, divided
3 slices American cheese
1/4 C. ketchup
2 tbsps chili-garlic sauce (such as Sriracha)
1 1/2 C. arugula
3 large eggs

Directions

1. Fill half pot with water and cook it until it starts boiling.
2. Add the ramen and cook it for 2 to 3 min until it become tender. Drain it and pace it aside.
3. Get a mixing bowl: Add the eggs with salt and pepper. Beat them well.
4. Fold in the noodles. Spoon the noodles into the 6 greased ramekins that are the size of burgers.
5. Place a piece of plastic on top then press them tightly to flatten them.
6. Place them in the fridge for 25 min to make the burger buns.
7. Get a mixing bowl: Add the beef, soy sauce, and sesame oil. Combine them well. Shape the mix into 3 burgers.
8. Place a large skillet on medium heat. Heat 1 tbsp of oil in it.
9. Add the refrigerated ramen buns and cook them for 4 min on each side until they become somewhat crunchy.
10. Drain the noodles buns and place them aside.
11. Heat another tbsp of oil in the same skillet.
12. Add the beef burgers and cook them for 8 min on each side.

13. Place a slice of cheese on each burger then cook it for 2.
14. Get a small mixing bowl: Add the ketchup and chili-garlic sauce. Combine them well.
15. Heat 1 tsp of oil in a large skillet. Cook in the 3 eggs. Season them with some salt and pepper. Spread the ketchup sauce in the inside of each ramen buns.
16. Top 2 ramen buns with arugula followed by the beef patties and fried eggs then cover them with the other 2 ramen buns. Serve your burgers right away. Enjoy.

BABY
Cheddar Burger

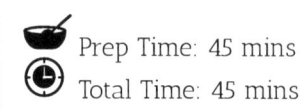

🥣 Prep Time: 45 mins
🕐 Total Time: 45 mins

Servings per Recipe: 5
Calories   624.1
Fat   16.9g
Cholesterol   242.0mg
Sodium   1702.9mg
Carbohydrates   95.0g
Protein   326.2g

Ingredients

1 kg potato, peeled
200 g of grated cheddar cheese
800 g frozen mixed vegetables (or fresh if you prefer)
1 Spanish onion
250 g golden breadcrumbs
Salt and pepper

Directions

1. Before you do anything preheat the oven to 400 F. Grease an oven proof grilling pan.
2. Bring a salted pot of water to a boil. Add the potato and cook it until it becomes soft. Place it aside to lose heat then mash it.
3. Get a mixing bowl: Add the mashed potato with onion, cheese, mixed veggies, salt and pepper. Divide the mix into 5 portions. Ask your kids to add mix them with their hands.
4. Shape them into burgers. Place a grill pan on medium heat. Place the burgers on the pan. Cook them in the oven for 20 min on each side.
5. Assemble your burgers with yours ad your kids' favorite toppings. Serve them right away.
6. Enjoy.

Rolled Kidney Bean Burgers

Prep Time: 15 mins
Total Time: 27 mins

Servings per Recipe: 1
Calories	301.9
Fat	3.1g
Cholesterol	0.0mg
Sodium	745.2mg
Carbohydrates	55.2g
Protein	114.6g

Ingredients

- 2 C. red kidney beans, drained, rinsed (from 19-oz can)
- 1/2 C. uncooked rolled oats
- 1/2 C. chopped fresh mushrooms
- 1/4 C. chopped onion
- 1 small carrot, shredded
- 1/2 medium red bell pepper, chopped
- 1 garlic clove, minced
- 2 tbsps ketchup
- 3/4 tsp salt
- 4 lettuce leaves
- 4 slices tomatoes
- 4 hamburger buns split

Directions

1. Before you do anything preheat the oven broiler.
2. Get a food processor: Add the beans, oats, mushrooms, onion, carrot, bell pepper, garlic, ketchup and salt. Mix them well until they become chopped. Form the mix into 4 burgers.
3. Grease a baking sheet. Place the burgers on it. Cook it in the oven broiler for 7 min on each side.
4. Assemble your burgers starting with a bun, lettuce, tomato, burger, ketchup and bun. Serve them right away.
5. Enjoy.

JALAPENO
Fritos Burger

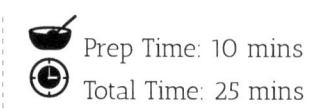

Prep Time: 10 mins
Total Time: 25 mins

Servings per Recipe: 8
Calories	681 kcal
Fat	40.3 g
Carbohydrates	27.3g
Protein	49.3 g
Cholesterol	196 mg
Sodium	936 mg

Ingredients

5 fresh jalapeno peppers
4 lbs ground beef
Salt and pepper to taste
1 egg
1/4 C. steak sauce, (e.g. Heinz 57)
1/4 C. minced white onion
1 tsp hot pepper sauce (e.g. Tabasco(TM))
1 pinch dried oregano
1 tbsp Worcestershire sauce
1 tsp garlic salt
1/4 C. crushed Fritos(R) corn chips
8 large potato hamburger buns
8 slices pepper jack cheese

Directions

1. Before you do anything preheat the grill.
2. Grill the jalapeno peppers for 3 to 4 min on each side. Wrap them in a piece of plastic and place them aside to sweat. Discard the flaky skin and seeds the chop them.
3. Get a large mixing bowl: Add the jalapenos, ground beef, salt, pepper, egg, steak sauce, onion, hot pepper sauce, oregano, Worcestershire sauce, garlic salt and Fritos. Mix them well.
4. Shape the mix into 8 burgers. Grill the burgers for 7 to 8 min on each side. Place the burgers in the buns with cheese slices while they are hot. Serve them right away.
5. Enjoy.

White Steak Burgers

Prep Time: 20 mins
Total Time: 30 mins

Servings per Recipe: 6
Calories   54.5
Fat   0.5g
Cholesterol   0.0mg
Sodium   65.6mg
Carbohydrates   9.1g
Protein   4.4g

Ingredients

- 1 lb. fresh mushrooms, about 6 C. chopped finely
- 1 large onion, minced
- 2 slices white bread, finely diced
- 2 tbsps steak sauce
- 2 egg whites or 1 egg
- Salt
- Ground black pepper

Directions

1. Place a large skillet on medium heat. Grease it with oil or cooking spray. Add the onion with mushroom and sauté them for 6 min. Add the bread dices with steak sauce. Sauté them for 1 min
2. Turn off the heat. Place the mix aside to lose heat.
3. Get a mixing bowl: Add the eggs and mix them well. Add the onion mix with salt and pepper. Mix them well. Shape the mix into 6 burgers.
4. Place a large skillet on medium heat. Heat in it a splash of oil. Add the burgers and cook them for 8 min on each side.
5. Assemble your burgers with your favorite toppings. Serve them right away.
6. Enjoy.

SOUPY Onion Burger

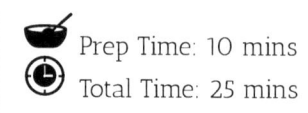

Prep Time: 10 mins
Total Time: 25 mins

Servings per Recipe: 6
Calories   371.8
Fat   26.1g
Cholesterol   111.8mg
Sodium   236.8mg
Carbohydrates   1.1g
Protein   30.8g

Ingredients

1 (1 oz.) envelope soup mix, onion
2 lbs ground beef
1/2 C. water

3/4 C. cheese (cheddar, mozzarella or Monterey jack)

Directions

1. Before you do anything preheat the grill.
2. Get a mixing bowl: Add all the ingredients and mix them well.
3. Shape the mix into 12 burgers. Place 2 tbsps of cheese in the middle of 6 burgers Top them with the remaining burgers and press the edges to seal them.
4. Cook the patties in the grill for 7 to 8 min on each side. Serve your burgers with your favorite toppings.
5. Enjoy.

Thai Bell Bean Burgers

🥣 Prep Time: 15 mins
🕐 Total Time: 35 mins

Servings per Recipe: 4
Calories   198 kcal
Fat   3 g
Carbohydrates   33.1g
Protein   11.2 g
Cholesterol   46 mg
Sodium   607 mg

Ingredients

- 1 (16 ounce) can black beans, drained and rinsed
- 1/2 green bell pepper, cut into 2 inch pieces
- 1/2 onion, cut into wedges
- 3 cloves garlic, peeled
- 1 egg
- 1 tbsp chili powder
- 1 tbsp cumin
- 1 tsp Thai chili sauce or hot sauce
- 1/2 C. bread crumbs

Directions

1. Before you do anything heat the grill and grease it.
2. Get a mixing bowl: Add the black bean then press it with a potato masher or fork until it becomes well mashed.
3. Get a food processor: Add the bell pepper, onion, and garlic. Mix them well. Add the black beans and blend them smooth.
4. Get a small bowl: Add the egg, chili powder, cumin, and chili sauce. Whisk them well to make the sauce. Add the black bean mix with bread crumbs. Mix them well.
5. Shape the mix into 4 burger cakes. Cook them on the grill for 9 min on each side. Assemble your burgers with your favorite toppings. Serve them right away.
6. Enjoy.

VIDALIA
Turkey Burgers

Prep Time: 30 mins
Total Time: 45 mins

Servings per Recipe: 4
Calories   788.1
Fat   16.0g
Cholesterol   109.8mg
Sodium   1190.4mg
Carbohydrates   94.4g
Protein   58.8g

Ingredients

1 1/4 lbs ground turkey breast or 1 1/2 lbs lean ground turkey
1/2 tsp kosher salt, plus more to taste
1/2-3/4 tsp fresh ground black pepper, plus more to taste
3 tbsps chicken broth
1 tbsp Dijon mustard
1/4 C. grated Vidalia onion
1 -2 garlic clove, minced
1 1/4 tsps thyme
1/2 tsp dried sage
1/3 C. breadcrumbs
3 oz. goat cheese
2 tbsps chicken broth

Vidalia Sauce
1 tbsp olive oil
1 large Vidalia onion, halved and cut into thin half rings
2 C. sliced cremini mushrooms
1/3-1/2 C. chicken broth
2 tsps butter
Toppings
4 roasted sweet red peppers, halves jarred
8 slices sourdough bread, sliced

Directions

1. Get a large mixing bowl: Add the lean turkey with salt, pepper, broth, Dijon mustard, garlic, grated onions, thyme, and sage. Combine them well.
2. Fold in the breadcrumbs.
3. Shape the mix into 8 burgers. Divide the cheese between 4 burgers and place it in the middle.
4. Cover them with the other 4 burgers and seal their edges by pressing them.
5. Place a large skillet on medium heat. Heat the olive oil in it.
6. Add the cook in it the onion for 6 min.
7. Stir in the broth with mushroom, salt and pepper then cook them for 4 min.
8. Stir in the butter and cook them for 1 min to make the sauce.

9. Put on the lid and turn off the heat. Place the sauce aside.
10. Place a large skillet on medium heat.
11. Heat in it a splash of oil. Add the turkey patties and cook them for 5 min on each side.
12. Stir in the remaining broth and cook them for another 3 min.
13. Toast the sourdough slices. Lay the roasted peppers on 4 bread slices then top them with the burgers, mushroom sauce and cover them with the remaining 4 bread slices.
14. Serve your burgers right away.
15. Enjoy.

SAUCY
Hot Winter Soup

Prep Time: 20 mins
Total Time: 1 hr 50 mins

Servings per Recipe: 8
Calories 216 kcal
Fat 5.8 g
Carbohydrates 20.3g
Protein 19.6 g
Cholesterol 45 mg
Sodium 550 mg

Ingredients

1 tbsp olive oil
1 1/2 lbs beef top sirloin, cut into bite-sized pieces
3 ribs celery, chopped
1 small onion, chopped
4 C. water
2 (14 oz.) cans beef broth
1 (14 oz.) can petite diced tomatoes
1 (14 oz.) can diced tomatoes
2 potatoes cut into bite-sized pieces
10 baby carrots, chopped
2 tsp garlic powder
2 small bay leaves
1 C. frozen corn
1 C. frozen green beans
2 tsp hot pepper sauce (such as Tabasco(R))

Directions

1. Place a large soup pot over medium heat. Add the oil and heat it. Add the beef and it for 6 min. drain it and place it aside.
2. Add the onion with celery to the pot and them for 6 min. Stir in the beef back with water, beef broth, petite diced tomatoes, diced tomatoes, potatoes, baby carrots, garlic powder, and bay leaves.
3. Put on the lid and the soup until it starts boiling. Lower the heat and remove the lid. The soup for 50 min
4. Add the rest of the ingredients. Put on the lid and the soup for 35 min.
5. Adjust the seasoning of the soup then serve it warm.
6. Enjoy.

Addictive Carrot Juice Soup

🍲 Prep Time: 10 mins
🕐 Total Time: 6 hrs 10 mins

Servings per Recipe: 6
Calories   364 kcal
Fat   16.2 g
Carbohydrates   38.8g
Protein   120 g
Cholesterol   51 mg
Sodium   1252 mg

Ingredients

1 lb cubed beef stew meat
1 (15.25 oz.) can whole kernel corn, undrained
1 (15 oz.) can green beans
1 (15 oz.) can carrots with juice
1 (15 oz.) can sliced potatoes with juice
1 (28 oz.) can crushed tomatoes
1 (1.25 oz.) package beef with onion soup mix
Salt and pepper to taste

Directions

1. Combine all the ingredients in a greased slow cooker. Put on the lid and it for 6 h 30 min on low.
2. Adjust the seasoning of the soup then serve it warm.
3. Enjoy.

TEX MEX
Turkey Soup

Prep Time: 15 mins
Total Time: 50 mins

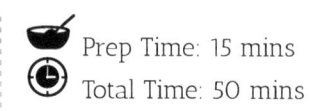

Servings per Recipe: 6
Calories   277 kcal
Fat   7.8 g
Carbohydrates   20g
Protein   29.6 g
Cholesterol   72 mg
Sodium   935 mg

Ingredients

1 lb lean ground beef
1 lb lean ground turkey
1/2 onion, chopped
1 1/2 C. water
2 (28 oz.) cans diced tomatoes
1 1/2 tsp garlic powder (such as Lawry's(R))
1 1/2 tsp sea salt, or to taste
1/2 tsp dried basil
1/2 tsp finely ground black pepper, or to taste

3 1/2 tsp beef base (such as Better Than Bouillon(R))
2 (12 oz.) packages frozen mixed vegetables

Directions

1. Place a soup pot over medium heat. Add the turkey with beef and them for 8 min. add the onion and them for 6 min. discard the grease.
2. Stir in the rest of the ingredients. The soup until it starts boiling. Lower the heat and simmer the soup for 25 min.
3. Adjust the seasoning of the soup then serve it warm.
4. Enjoy.

Hot and Sweet Soup

Prep Time: 25 mins
Total Time: 6 hrs 30 mins

Servings per Recipe: 4
Calories   205 kcal
Fat   6.6 g
Carbohydrates   24g
Protein   13.7 g
Cholesterol   26 mg
Sodium   429 mg

Ingredients

- 3 tbsp vegetable oil
- 2 tbsp all-purpose flour
- 1 1/2 lbs beef stew meat, trimmed
- 1 (32 oz.) carton beef stock
- 4 C. hot water
- 2 C. fresh green beans cut into bite-sized pieces
- 1 (15 oz.) can tomato sauce
- 1 (14.5 oz.) can stewed tomatoes
- 4 carrots, sliced into circles
- 4 potatoes cut into large dice
- 1 1/2 C. fresh corn kernels
- 1 C. chopped celery
- 1 yellow onion, diced
- 1/2 C. sweet peas
- 4 tsp beef bouillon granules
- 3 tbsp dried parsley
- 2 bay leaves
- 1 tsp thyme
- 1/2 tsp chili powder
- 1/2 tsp ground black pepper

Directions

1. Get a mixing bowl: Place in it the flour. Season the beef with some salt and pepper. Coat it with the flour.
2. Place a soup over medium heat. Heat the oil in it. Add the beef and brown in it for 6 min. Stir in the rest of the ingredients.
3. Put on the lid and lower the heat. Simmer the soup for 6 min while stirring it occasionally.
4. Adjust the seasoning of the soup then serve it warm.
5. Enjoy.

MARJORAM
Liver Soup

Prep Time: 15 mins
Total Time: 1 hr

Servings per Recipe: 4
Calories   1008 kcal
Fat   68.3 g
Carbohydrates   40g
Protein   156.5 g
Cholesterol   1451 mg
Sodium   153355 mg

Ingredients

- 1 C. ground chicken liver
- 1 C. dried bread crumbs
- 3 tbsp all-purpose flour
- 2 eggs
- 1/4 tbsp chopped fresh parsley
- 1 tsp salt
- 1/8 tsp dried marjoram
- 1/8 tsp ground allspice
- 1 clove garlic, minced
- 2 lbs short rib steaks
- 2 onions, thinly sliced
- 3 stalks chopped celery, with leaves
- 4 tsp salt
- 3/4 tsp ground black pepper
- 8 C. water
- 2 carrots, halved
- 3 tomatoes, chopped
- 4 sprigs fresh parsley

Directions

1. Get a mixing bowl: Add the liver, bread crumbs, flour, eggs, parsley, 1 tsp salt, marjoram, allspice, and garlic. Combine them well. Place the mix aside.
2. Place a large soup over medium heat. Add the rest of the ingredients. Put on the lid and the soup until it starts boiling. Lower the heat and the soup for 1 h 35 min.
3. Drain the carrot the meat. Cut into small pieces. Stir them back into the pot and it until it start boiling.
4. Form the liver mix into meatballs and stir them into the soup. The soup over medium heat for 10 min
5. Adjust the seasoning of the soup then serve it warm.
6. Enjoy.

Lime Beef Soup

Prep Time: 15 mins
Total Time: 40 mins

Servings per Recipe: 6
Calories	359 kcal
Fat	11.7 g
Carbohydrates	36.5g
Protein	128.3 g
Cholesterol	50 mg
Sodium	1881 mg

Ingredients

- 1 lb beef shank
- 1 tomato, quartered
- 2 potatoes, cubed
- 1 onion, chopped
- 3 carrots, chopped
- 1/2 medium head cabbage, chopped
- 4 cloves garlic, minced
- 6 tsp chopped fresh cilantro
- 1 tbsp salt
- 1/4 tsp ground cumin
- 2 fluid oz. fresh lime juice

Directions

1. Place a soup pot over low heat. Add the beef, tomato, potatoes, onion, carrots, cabbage, garlic, 5 tsp cilantro, salt and cumin.
2. Cover them with water. Put on the lid and the soup for 2 h 10 min.
3. Remove the cover and the soup for 1 h 5 min while stirring occasionally. Serve the soup hot with the rest of the cilantro and lime juice.
4. Enjoy.

CHUNKY MESSY
Garden Soup

Prep Time: 30 mins
Total Time: 12 hrs 30 mins

Servings per Recipe: 4
Calories   260 kcal
Fat   10.6 g
Carbohydrates   20.6 g
Protein   17.3 g
Cholesterol   40 mg
Sodium   570 mg

Ingredients

1 C. dry mixed beans
1 1/2 lbs cubed beef stew meat
5 C. beef broth
1 C. vegetable broth
1 (28 oz.) can whole peeled tomatoes
4 large carrots cut into 2 inch pieces
3 stalks celery, cut into 2 inch pieces
3 potatoes, peeled and cubed
3 cloves garlic, minced
4 green onions, chopped
1 tsp salt

1 tsp ground black pepper
1 tsp ground cayenne pepper
1/2 tsp crushed red pepper flakes
1 tbsp dried oregano
1 tbsp ground dry mustard
1 dash hot sauce

Directions

1. Transfer the mixed beans to a large saucepan. Cover them water adding 2 inches on top. They until they start rolling boil. Keep boiling them for 12 min.
2. Turn off the heat. Place the beans with the lid on for 2 h 15 min. Rinse the beans and drain them.
3. Transfer the beans with the rest of ingredients to a slow cooker. Put on the lid and the soup for 11 h.
4. Adjust the seasoning of the soup then serve it warm.
5. Enjoy.

Black Pea Sirloin Soup

Prep Time: 15 mins
Total Time: 8 hrs 15 mins

Servings per Recipe: 4
Calories   354 kcal
Fat   10.4 g
Carbohydrates   45.9 g
Protein   122.4 g
Cholesterol   46 mg
Sodium   1465 mg

Ingredients

- 1 (32 fluid oz.) container beef broth or more if needed
- 1 lb ground sirloin beef
- 1 (15.25 oz.) can whole kernel corn, drained
- 1 (15 oz.) can green beans, drained
- 1 (15 oz.) can peas, drained
- 1 (14 oz.) can tomato sauce
- 3 carrots cut into bite-size pieces
- 2 potatoes, peeled and cut into bite-size pieces
- 1 onion, chopped
- 1 large stalk celery, cut into bite-size pieces
- 1 clove garlic, minced
- 1 1/2 tbsp chopped fresh parsley
- 1/2 tsp celery seed
- 2 bay leaves
- Salt and ground black pepper to taste

Directions

1. Combine all the ingredients in a slow cooker. Put on the lid and them for 8 h on low while adding more broth if needed.
2. Adjust the seasoning of the soup then serve it warm.
3. Enjoy.

CONSOMMÉ
Jungle Soup

Prep Time: 20 mins
Total Time: 6 hrs 20 mins

Servings per Recipe: 6
Calories	293 kcal
Fat	8.4 g
Carbohydrates	33.4g
Protein	122.4 g
Cholesterol	37 mg
Sodium	814 mg

Ingredients

- 3/4 lb beef stew meat, cut into 1 inch cubes
- 2 onions, diced
- 3 cloves garlic, minced
- 1 large stalk celery, minced
- 2 carrots, finely chopped
- 1/4 lb green beans cut into 1 inch pieces
- 8 oz. fresh mushrooms, coarsely chopped
- 3 potatoes, peeled and diced
- 1 (14.5 oz.) can crushed tomatoes
- 1 (8 oz.) can tomato sauce
- 1 bay leaf
- 1/2 tsp ground black pepper
- 1/2 tsp dried thyme
- 1/4 tsp dried marjoram
- 2 (14.5 oz.) cans fat-free chicken broth
- 1/2 C. all-purpose flour
- 2 (10.5 oz.) cans beef consommé

Directions

1. Combine all the ingredients in a slow cooker. Stir them well.
2. Put on the lid and the soup for 8 h on low. Adjust the seasoning of the soup then serve it warm.
3. Enjoy.

Italian Worcestershire Soup

Prep Time: 15 mins
Total Time: 7 hrs 25 mins

Servings per Recipe: 6
Calories   264 kcal
Fat   7.9 g
Carbohydrates   30.5g
Protein   11.8 g
Cholesterol   34 mg
Sodium   1504 mg

Ingredients

1 lb ground beef
2 cloves garlic, minced
1 small onion, diced
1 green bell pepper, diced
3 stalks celery, diced
1 (29 oz.) can Italian-style stewed tomatoes, drained
1 (15 oz.) can mixed vegetables, drained

2 quarts beef broth
3 tbsp soy sauce
2 tbsp Worcestershire sauce
3/4 tsp paprika
Salt and pepper to taste
6 oz. dry fusilli pasta

Directions

1. Place a large skillet over medium heat. Add the beef with garlic, onion, and green bell pepper. Those for 6 min. discard the grease.
2. Place the mix into a greased slow cooker with the rest of the ingredients except for the pasta and stir them. Put on the lid and the soup for 7 h 15 min on low.
3. Add the pasta and the soup for 16 min on low. Adjust the seasoning of the soup then serve it warm.
4. Enjoy.

BELL
Green Beef Soup

🍲 Prep Time: 20 mins
🕐 Total Time: 5hrs 20 mins

Servings per Recipe: 6
Calories	186.7
Fat	4.6 g
Cholesterol	17.5 mg
Sodium	1012.7 mg
Carbohydrates	29.6 g
Protein	9 g

Ingredients

- 1/3 lb ground beef
- 1/2 C. onion, chopped
- 1/4 C. celery, chopped
- 1/4 C. green pepper, chopped
- 2 garlic cloves, pressed
- 2 carrots, sliced
- 2 medium potatoes, cubed
- 1 zucchini, sliced & quartered
- 1 C. green beans, pieces
- 1 (28 oz.) can crushed tomatoes
- 2 bay leaves
- 1 tsp basil
- 1 tsp oregano
- 1 tsp thyme
- 2 tsp parsley
- 1/2 tbsp sugar
- 1 tbsp Worcestershire sauce
- 4 beef bouillon cubes
- 2 chicken bouillon cubes
- 3 C. water

Directions

1. Place a large crockpot over medium heat. Add the beef with onion, celery, green pepper, and garlic. Them for 8 min
2. Pour the water in a large saucepan and it until it starts boiling. Add the beef & chicken bouillon then stir them well. Transfer the mix to the soup pot.
3. Put on the lid and the soup for 2 h 30 min on high or 5 h on low.
4. Adjust the seasoning of the soup then serve it warm.
5. Enjoy.

Tabasco Soup

Prep Time: 30 mins
Total Time: 2 hrs 30 mins

Servings per Recipe: 8
Calories	339.6
Fat	16.2 g
Cholesterol	59.8 mg
Sodium	648.2 mg
Carbohydrates	27.4 g
Protein	22.5 g

Ingredients

- 1 lb beef stew meat
- 3 onions, chopped
- 6 carrots, diced
- 1 lb button mushroom, sliced
- 8 C. beef broth (use low If you prefer)
- 1 C. barley
- 1 tsp garlic salt
- 1 tsp dried basil
- 1/4 tsp pepper
- 2 dashes Tabasco sauce

Directions

1. Trim the beef stew meat from the fat.
2. Heat a splash of olive oil in a large soup pot. Add the beef and it for 4 min.
3. Add the rest of the ingredients and stir them. The soup until it starts boiling. Lower the heat and the soup for 2 h 10 min. Adjust the seasoning of the soup then serve it warm.
4. Enjoy.

ASIAN
Anise Soup

Prep Time: 25 mins
Total Time: 2 hrs 40 mins

Servings per Recipe: 6
Calories   410.5
Fat   25.1 g
Cholesterol   106.6 mg
Sodium   2910.8 mg
Carbohydrates   11.2 g
Protein   33.7 g

Ingredients

1/2 C. gingerroot, thinly sliced
1 C. shallot, thinly sliced
1 tsp anise seed or 3 star anise, whole
1 cinnamon stick
1 1/2 lbs beef chuck, boned, rinsed and fat trimmed
2 1/4 quarts beef broth
1/4 C. fish sauce (Nouc Mam)
1 tbsp sugar
1/8 tsp salt
2 tbsp Southeast Asian fish sauce
2 C. bean sprouts, rinsed (optional)
1/4 C. jalapeno chile, thinly sliced (optional)
1/2 C. Thai basil, rinsed (optional)
1/2 C. fresh cilantro, rinsed (optional)
3 limes, rinsed and cut into wedges (optional)
8 oz. sirloin steaks, fat trimmed, very thinly sliced
6 C. cooked rice vermicelli
1/2 C. yellow onion, thinly sliced
3/4 C. green onion, thinly sliced (including tops)
Hoisin sauce (optional)
fish sauce (optional)

Directions

1. Place 2 layers of cheesecloth on a working space. Place in the middle of it ginger, anise, shallots and cinnamon. Wrap the cloth around them and tie them with a cotton string.
2. Place a large soup pot over high heat. Add the beef chuck, broth, 2 1/2 qts water, nouc mam sauce, sugar and spice bundle. Drain the meat and freeze it.
3. Put on the lid and them until they start boiling. Turn off the heat and place the soup aside to lose heat. Place the soup in the fridge and let it set for an overnight.
4. Cut the frozen meat into thin slices. Remove the fat the rose on top of the soup in the pot.
5. Stir in 1/8 tsp salt and 2 tbsp Nouc Mam sauce then it on medium heat until it starts boiling. Lower the heat and add the beef slices. It for 1 min then drains it and places it aside.
6. Divide the rice between 6 serving bowl then top them with the beef slices, sirloin, yellow onion and green onions. Pour the hot soup on top then serve them right away.
7. Enjoy.

Classic French Soup

🥣 Prep Time: 10 mins
🕐 Total Time: 1 hr 10 mins

Servings per Recipe: 6
Calories 196.9
Fat 11.9 g
Cholesterol 41 mg
Sodium 675.4 mg
Carbohydrates 12.3 g
Protein 10.4 g

Ingredients

4 C. thinly sliced onions
3 tbsp butter or 3 tbsp s margarine
1 tbsp soy sauce
1/2 lb ground beef
2 tbsp s flour
1 tsp celery salt
1/2 tsp pepper
1/2 tsp garlic powder
4 C. beef broth or 4 C. beef bouillon
Parmesan cheese

Directions

1. Place a soup pot over heat. Add the butter and melt it. Stir in the onion and it for 32 while stirring it often.
2. Stir in the beef with soy sauce. Put on the lid and those for 16 min. add the rest of the ingredients and them until they start boiling.
3. Lower the heat and the soup for 6 min. adjust the seasoning of the soup then serve it warm.
4. Enjoy.

QUINOA
Festival

Prep Time: 5 mins
Total Time: 40 mins

Servings per Recipe: 2
Calories 473 kcal
Fat 19.8 g
Carbohydrates 62.8g
Protein 13.5 g
Cholesterol 0 mg
Sodium 48 mg

Ingredients

2 tbsps olive oil, or as needed
1 small onion, diced
2 cloves garlic, minced
1 C. quinoa
2 C. chicken broth

1 tbsp curry powder, or to taste
1 tbsp ancho chili powder
salt and pepper to taste

Directions

1. Stir fry your garlic and onions in oil for 4 mins then add your quinoa and cook for 6 mins.
2. Add in the broth and get everything boiling. Once the quinoa is boiling, add your chili and curry powder, place a lid on the pot, and lower the heat. Let the contents cook for 27 mins.
3. Before serving add your preferred amount of pepper and salt.
4. Enjoy.

Chicken, Cucumbers, and Parsley Couscous

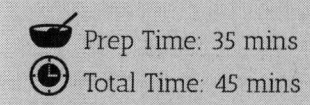

Prep Time: 35 mins
Total Time: 45 mins

Servings per Recipe: 6
Calories	645 kcal
Fat	38.8 g
Carbohydrates	44g
Protein	29.4 g
Cholesterol	68 mg
Sodium	792 mg

Ingredients

- 2 C. chicken broth
- 1 (10 oz.) box couscous
- 3/4 C. olive oil
- 1/4 C. fresh lemon juice
- 2 tbsps white balsamic vinegar
- 1/4 C. chopped fresh rosemary leaves
- salt and ground black pepper to taste
- 2 large cooked skinless, boneless chicken breast halves, cut into bite-size pieces
- 1 C. chopped English cucumber
- 1/2 C. chopped sun-dried tomatoes
- 1/2 C. chopped pitted kalamata olives
- 1/2 C. crumbled feta cheese
- 1/3 C. chopped fresh Italian parsley
- salt and ground black pepper to taste

Directions

1. Get your stock boiling then add in your couscous.
2. Place a lid on the pot and shut the heat.
3. Let the contents sit for 7 mins before stirring.
4. Blend: vinegar, olive oil, and lemon juice with some rosemary.
5. Now add some pepper and salt before continuing.
6. Get a bowl, mix: tomatoes, parsley, couscous, feta, cucumbers, and chicken.
7. Cover the couscous with the dressing and add a bit more if you like also add some more pepper and salt too.
8. Enjoy.

LIME and Chicken Couscous

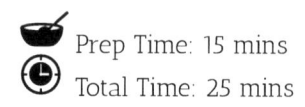

Prep Time: 15 mins
Total Time: 25 mins

Servings per Recipe: 4
Calories   380 kcal
Fat   6.2 g
Carbohydrates   52g
Protein   28.4 g
Cholesterol   59 mg
Sodium   1675 mg

Ingredients

1 tbsp olive oil
1 lb skinless, boneless chicken breast halves, cubed
1 pinch monosodium glutamate (MSG)
6 tbsps soy sauce
6 tbsps brown sugar
1/2 tsp red pepper flakes, or more to taste
1 lime, juiced and zested
2 C. vegetable broth
1 C. couscous
1/3 C. chopped cilantro
4 wedges lime for garnish

Directions

1. Get a bowl, combine: zest, soy sauce, lime juice, sugar, and pepper flakes.
2. Boil everything gently for 4 mins until it becomes sauce like.
3. Now stir fry your chicken until it is fully done in olive oil for 7 mins.
4. Add in your MSG while it fries.
5. Then top everything with the lime sauce and continue stir frying for 4 more mins.
6. Let your couscous sit in the veggie broth that was boiling for 7 mins in a covered pot.
7. Place some couscous on a plate for serving and add a topping of lime chicken.
8. Garnish with freshly squeezed lime from the wedges.
9. Enjoy.

Peppers, Corn, and Black Beans Couscous

Prep Time: 30 mins
Total Time: 35 mins

Servings per Recipe: 8
Calories	255 kcal
Fat	5.9 g
Carbohydrates	41.2g
Protein	10.4 g
Cholesterol	< 1 mg
Sodium	565 mg

Ingredients

- 1 C. uncooked couscous
- 1 1/4 C. chicken broth
- 3 tbsps extra virgin olive oil
- 2 tbsps fresh lime juice
- 1 tsp balsamic vinegar
- 1/2 tsp ground cumin
- 8 green onions, chopped
- 1 red bell pepper, seeded and chopped
- 1/4 C. chopped fresh cilantro
- 1 C. frozen corn kernels, thawed
- 2 (15 oz.) cans black beans, drained
- salt and pepper to taste

Directions

1. Get your broth boiling for 2 mins then add in your couscous.
2. Place a lid on the pot and shut the heat.
3. Let the couscous sit in the hot water for 7 mins, before stirring it.
4. Get a bowl, mix: beans, olive oil, couscous, corn, lime juice, cilantro, vinegar, red pepper, onions, and cumin.
5. Add your preferred amount of pepper and salt. Then place a plastic covering around the bowl, let the mix sit in the fridge for 20 to 30 mins before serving.
6. Enjoy.

CREAMY PARSLEY, Chickpeas, and Almonds Couscous

Prep Time: 15 mins
Total Time: 1 hr 45 mins

Servings per Recipe: 6
Calories   247 kcal
Fat   12.2 g
Carbohydrates   30g
Protein   5.7 g
Cholesterol   13 mg
Sodium   251 mg

Ingredients

1/2 C. creamy salad dressing
1/4 C. plain yogurt
1 tsp ground cumin
salt and pepper to taste
1 tbsp butter
1/2 C. couscous
1 C. water
1 red onion, chopped

1 red bell pepper, chopped
1/3 C. chopped parsley
1/3 C. raisins
1/3 C. toasted and sliced almonds
1/2 C. canned chickpeas, drained

Directions

1. Get a bowl, combine: pepper, salad dressing, salt, cumin, and yogurt.
2. Cover the bowl with some plastic wrap and chill in the fridge for 1 h.
3. Simultaneously toast your couscous in butter for 2 mins then add your water.
4. Get everything boiling, then place a lid on the pot, set the heat to low and let the contents gently boil for 7 mins.
5. Get your dressing mix and add in: chickpeas, couscous, almonds, red onions, raisins, parsley, and bell peppers.
6. Place the covering back on the bowl and put it back in the fridge for 20 mins.
7. Enjoy.

Veggie Turkey Couscous Bits Couscous

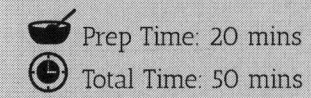

Prep Time: 20 mins
Total Time: 50 mins

Servings per Recipe: 10
Calories   119 kcal
Fat   1 g
Carbohydrates   13.6 g
Protein   13.2 g
Cholesterol   47 mg
Sodium   244 mg

Ingredients

- 2 C. coarsely chopped zucchini
- 1 1/2 C. coarsely chopped onions
- 1 red bell pepper, coarsely chopped
- 1 lb extra lean ground turkey
- 1/2 C. uncooked couscous
- 1 egg
- 2 tbsps Worcestershire sauce
- 1 tbsp Dijon mustard
- 1/2 C. barbecue sauce, or as needed

Directions

1. Coat your muffin pan with non-stick spray and then set your oven to 400 degrees before doing anything else.
2. Blend with a few pulses: bell peppers, zucchini, and onions. Then add them to a bowl, with: mustard, turkey, Worcestershire, eggs, and couscous.
3. Evenly divide the mix between the sections in your muffin pan then add bbq sauce to each (1 tsp).
4. Cook everything in the oven for 27 mins.
5. Check the temperature of each, it should be 160 degrees.
6. Let the dish sit for 10 mins before serving.
7. Enjoy.

SQUASH and Garbanzos Couscous (Moroccan Style III)

Prep Time: 15 mins
Total Time: 1 hr

Servings per Recipe: 4
Calories   502 kcal
Fat   11.7 g
Carbohydrates   93.8g
Protein   11.2 g
Cholesterol   10 mg
Sodium   728 mg

Ingredients

2 tbsps brown sugar
1 tbsp butter, melted
2 large acorn squash, halved and seeded
2 tbsps olive oil
2 cloves garlic, chopped
2 stalks celery, chopped
2 carrots, chopped

1 C. garbanzo beans, drained
1/2 C. raisins
1 1/2 tbsps ground cumin
salt and pepper to taste
1 (14 oz.) can chicken broth
1 C. uncooked couscous

Directions

1. Set your oven to 350 degrees before doing anything else.
2. Cook your squash for 32 mins in the oven. Then top the squash with a mix of butter and sugar that has been melted and stirred together.
3. Stir fry, for 7 mins, in olive oil: carrots, celery, and garlic.
4. Now add the raisins and beans.
5. Fry the contents until everything is soft then add in pepper, salt, and cumin. Add the broth to the carrot mix and then add the couscous.
6. Place a lid on the pot and place the pot to the side away from all heat.
7. Let the contents sit for 7 mins.
8. Fill your squashes with the couscous mix.
9. Enjoy.

Cherry Tomatoes, Onions, and Basil Couscous

Prep Time: 5 mins
Total Time: 40 mins

Servings per Recipe: 4
Calories	299 kcal
Fat	12.4 g
Carbohydrates	38g
Protein	9.1 g
Cholesterol	6 mg
Sodium	196 mg

Ingredients

- 1 C. couscous
- 1 C. boiling water
- 3 tbsps olive oil
- 1 clove garlic, minced
- 1/4 C. diced red bell pepper
- 4 green onions, sliced
- 1 C. cherry tomatoes
- 1 C. fresh basil leaves
- 1 pinch salt
- 1 pinch ground black pepper
- 1 dash balsamic vinegar
- 1/4 C. grated Parmesan cheese

Directions

1. Set your oven to 350 degrees before doing anything else.
2. Get your water boiling then pour in your couscous.
3. Get everything boiling again. Then place a lid on the pot, shut the heat, and let the mix sit for 7 mins before stirring.
4. Simultaneously stir fry your peppers, onions, and garlic for 3 mins then add: pepper, tomatoes, salt, basil, and couscous.
5. Pour everything into a baking dish and add in your balsamic.
6. Cook everything in the oven for 25 mins then add the parmesan.
7. Enjoy.

CHIPOTLE
Quinoa

Prep Time: 30 mins
Total Time: 1 hr

Servings per Recipe: 10
Calories   233 kcal
Fat   3.5 g
Carbohydrates   42g
Protein   11.5 g
Cholesterol   0 mg
Sodium   540 mg

Ingredients

1 C. uncooked quinoa, rinsed
2 C. water
1 tbsp vegetable oil
1 onion, chopped
4 cloves garlic, chopped
1 tbsp chili powder
1 tbsp ground cumin
1 (28 oz.) can crushed tomatoes
2 (19 oz.) cans black beans, rinsed and drained
1 green bell pepper, chopped
1 red bell pepper, chopped
1 zucchini, chopped
1 jalapeno pepper, seeded and minced
1 tbsp minced chipotle peppers in adobo sauce
1 tsp dried oregano
salt and ground black pepper to taste
1 C. frozen corn
1/4 C. chopped fresh cilantro

Directions

1. Boil your quinoa in water, then place a lid on the pot, lower the heat, and let the contents gently boil for 17 mins.
2. Simultaneously, in veggie oil, stir fry your onions for 7 mins then season them with: cumin, chili powder, and garlic.
3. Cook for 2 more mins before adding: oregano, tomatoes, chipotles, black beans, jalapenos, bell peppers, and zucchini.
4. Add in your preferred amount of black pepper and salt and get the contents to a gentle boil with high then low heat.
5. Place a lid on the pot and let the contents gently cook for 22 mins.
6. Now pour in your corn and quinoa and heat for 7 more mins before shutting the heat and topping with some cilantro.
7. Enjoy.

Mangos, and Salsa Couscous

Prep Time: 10 mins
Total Time: 20 mins

Servings per Recipe: 4
Calories	186 kcal
Fat	0.9 g
Carbohydrates	40.2g
Protein	5.1 g
Cholesterol	0 mg
Sodium	314 mg

Ingredients

- 1 1/2 C. water
- 1 C. couscous
- 2/3 C. dried mango, diced
- 3/4 C. prepared salsa
- 2 tsps ground cumin
- 1 tsp curry powder

Directions

1. Get the following boiling in a big pot: curry, couscous, water, cumin, mango, and salsa.
2. Place a lid on the pot and set the heat to low.
3. Cook everything for 4 mins and then let the contents sit for 7 more mins. Stir the couscous before plating.
4. Enjoy.

QUINOA
Summer Salad

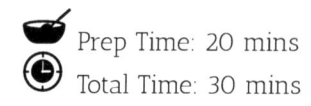

Prep Time: 20 mins
Total Time: 30 mins

Servings per Recipe: 6
Calories   270 kcal
Fat   11.5 g
Carbohydrates   33.8g
Protein   8.9 g
Cholesterol   0 mg
Sodium   739 mg

Ingredients

1 C. quinoa
2 C. water
1/4 C. extra-virgin olive oil
2 limes, juiced
2 tsps ground cumin
1 tsp salt
1/2 tsp red pepper flakes, or more to taste

1 1/2 C. halved cherry tomatoes
1 (15 oz.) can black beans, drained and rinsed
5 green onions, finely chopped
1/4 C. chopped fresh cilantro
salt and ground black pepper to taste

Directions

1. Boil your quinoa in water then place a lid on the pot, lower the heat, and let it cook for 17 mins.
2. Get a bowl, mix: red pepper, black pepper, olive oil, salt (1 tsp), cilantro, cumin, and lime juice.
3. Get a 2nd bowl, mix: onions, cooked quinoa, beans, and tomatoes.
4. Combine both bowls and toss the contents.
5. Enjoy.

Moroccan Salmon Cake Couscous

Prep Time: 20 mins
Total Time: 45 mins

Servings per Recipe: 4
Calories   620 kcal
Fat   46.4 g
Carbohydrates   26.4g
Protein   28.8 g
Cholesterol   178 mg
Sodium   950 mg

Ingredients

1/2 C. mayonnaise
1 clove garlic, crushed
1/8 tsp paprika
Salmon Cake:
1/2 C. couscous
2/3 C. orange juice
1 (14.75 oz.) can red salmon, drained
1 (10 oz.) package frozen chopped spinach, thawed, drained and squeezed dry
2 egg yolks, beaten
2 cloves garlic, crushed
1 tsp ground cumin
1/2 tsp ground black pepper
1/2 tsp salt
3 tbsps olive oil

Directions

1. Get a bowl, mix: paprika, mayo, and garlic.
2. Boil your orange juice in a large pot, then add in your couscous.
3. Get the mix boiling again and then place a lid on the pot, shut the heat, and let the couscous stand for 7 mins.
4. Now stir your couscous after it has lost all of its heat.
5. Get a 2nd bowl, combine: salt, salmon, black pepper, spinach, cumin, egg yolks, and garlic.
6. Shape this mix into patties and then fry them in olive oil for 8 mins turning each at 4 mins.
7. When serving add a topping of mayo.
8. Enjoy.

RUSTIC
Quinoa

Prep Time: 15 mins
Total Time: 1 hr 35 mins

Servings per Recipe: 6
Calories 379 kcal
Fat 26.9 g
Carbohydrates 25.6 g
Protein 9.9 g
Cholesterol 19 mg
Sodium 552 mg

Ingredients

1/2 lb beets, peeled and sliced
1 C. red quinoa
2 C. water
1/2 C. olive oil
1/2 C. balsamic vinegar
1 1/2 tsps white sugar
1 clove garlic, crushed

1 tsp salt
1/4 tsp ground black pepper
2 green onions, sliced
3 oz. arugula, chopped
5 oz. goat cheese, crumbled

Directions

1. Steam your beets over 2 inches of water for 12 mins with a steamer insert and a big pot.
2. Now boil your quinoa in 2 C. of water and then place a lid on the pot, lower the heat, and cook everything for 17 mins.
3. Get a bowl, combine: pepper, olive oil, salt, vinegar, garlic, and sugar.
4. Before stirring your quinoa pour in half of the wet mix. Then stir the quinoa.
5. Add everything to a bowl and then place this in the fridge for 1 hour with a covering of plastic wrap.
6. Once the quinoa has cooled add the following to it: beets, onions, cheese, and arugula.
7. Stir the mix and then add your dressing and stir again.
8. Enjoy chilled.

Pecans, Parmesan, and Pesto Couscous

Prep Time: 20 mins
Total Time: 50 mins

Servings per Recipe: 4
Calories	471 kcal
Fat	31.3 g
Carbohydrates	38.8g
Protein	11.3 g
Cholesterol	19 mg
Sodium	222 mg

Ingredients

- 2/3 C. pecan pieces
- 1 tbsp butter
- 1 1/2 C. quartered fresh button mushrooms
- 1 onion, chopped
- 1 tbsp minced fresh garlic
- 2 tsps butter
- 1 1/4 C. water
- 1 (5.8 oz.) box couscous
- 1 (8.5 oz.) bottle sun-dried tomato pesto
- 1/3 C. finely grated Parmesan cheese, or more to taste
- salt and ground black pepper to taste

Directions

1. Toast your pecans in the oven in a casserole dish for 25 mins.
2. Meanwhile stir fry the garlic, onions, and mushrooms in 1 tbsp of butter for 9 mins. Then place it all in a bowl.
3. Melt 2 more tbsp of butter and then add in your water get it boiling.
4. Once everything is boiling add your couscous to a big bowl and then combine it with the boiling water.
5. Place a covering on the bowl of plastic wrap and let it sit for 12 mins.
6. After all the liquid has been absorbed stir it with a fork.
7. Add the pesto, pecans, parmesan, and mushrooms to the couscous and then add some pepper and salt.
8. Mix everything evenly.
9. Enjoy.

LUNCHTIME
Quinoa

🍲 Prep Time: 15 mins
🕐 Total Time: 30 mins

Servings per Recipe: 8
Calories   387
Fat   9.8g
Cholesterol   0mg
Sodium   258mg
Carbohydrates   70.7g
Protein   9.1g

Ingredients

4 C. vegetable broth
2 C. uncooked quinoa
¼ C. olive oil
2 small zucchinis, cubed into 1-inch size
1 butternut squash, peeled, seeded and chopped
1 C. dried cranberries
1 C. dried apricots
1 C. fresh parsley, chopped
1 bunch scallion, chopped
2 tbsp fresh lime juice

Directions

1. In a pan, add broth and bring to a boil.
2. Stir in quinoa and immediately, reduce the heat to low.
3. Simmer, covered for about 10-15 minutes or till all the liquid is absorbed. Remove from heat and keep aside.
4. In a large skillet, heat oil on medium heat.
5. Add zucchini and squash and cook for about 10 minutes.
6. Stir in cooked quinoa juice, dried fruit, parsley and scallion.
7. Serve with the drizzling of lime juice.

Honey Rutabaga Couscous

Prep Time: 15 mins
Total Time: 35 mins

Servings per Recipe: 6
Calories	330 kcal
Fat	12.3 g
Carbohydrates	44.2g
Protein	11.7 g
Cholesterol	0 mg
Sodium	89 mg

Ingredients

- 1 rutabaga, chunked
- 2 C. water
- 1 tbsp vegetable oil
- 1 1/2 C. couscous
- 1/2 C. nutritional yeast
- 1/4 C. vegetable oil
- 1/4 C. apple cider vinegar
- 1 1/2 tsps honey
- 1 tsp Italian seasoning
- 1 tsp dried oregano
- 1 tsp dried dill weed
- 1/2 tsp ground black pepper
- 1/4 tsp cayenne pepper
- 1 pinch salt to taste (optional)

Directions

1. Steam your rutabaga over 2 inches of boiling water for 12 mins with a steamer insert.
2. Boil 1 tbsp of veggie oil with 2 C. of water then add in the couscous and shut the heat after placing a lid on the pot.
3. Let this sit for 15 mins before stirring after it has cooled.
4. Get a bowl, combine: cayenne, veggie oil, black pepper, vinegar, dill, honey, oregano, and Italian seasonings.
5. Add the rutabaga, couscous, and some salt to the dressing mix.
6. Toss the contents to coat everything evenly.
7. Enjoy.

QUINOA
Classico

🥣 Prep Time: 10 mins
🕐 Total Time: 30 mins

Servings per Recipe: 6
Calories   157 kcal
Fat   4.7 g
Carbohydrates   21.8 g
Protein   6.5 g
Cholesterol   8 mg
Sodium   97 mg

Ingredients

- 1 tbsp butter
- 1 C. uncooked quinoa
- 2 C. chicken broth
- 1/4 C. chopped onion
- 1 clove garlic, minced
- 1 tsp chopped fresh thyme
- 1/2 tsp black pepper
- 3/4 C. frozen peas
- 1/2 C. grated Pecorino Romano cheese
- 2 tbsps chopped fresh parsley

Directions

1. Toast your quinoa for 3 mins in butter then add: pepper, broth, thyme, garlic, and onions.
2. Get the mix boiling then add in the peas, place a lid on the pot, lower the heat, and let the mix cook for 17 mins.
3. Now add in your parsley and Romano then stir the contents.
4. Place the quinoa in a bowl and top with some more cheese.
5. Enjoy.

Mexican
Pineapple and Beans Couscous

Prep Time: 10 mins
Total Time: 25 mins

Servings per Recipe: 2
Calories   675 kcal
Fat   1.3 g
Carbohydrates   141.2g
Protein   24.7 g
Cholesterol   0 mg
Sodium   1486 mg

Ingredients

1/2 C. water
1 (15 oz.) can pineapple chunks, drained (juice reserved)
1 C. couscous
1 (15 oz.) can black beans, rinsed and drained
1/3 C. warm water
2 tbsps taco seasoning mix

Directions

1. Boil .5 C. of water along with the pineapple juice then add in your couscous and place a lid on the pot after shutting the heat.
2. Let the couscous sit for 7 mins before stirring it.
3. Stir fry the beans and pineapple with taco seasoning and 1/3 C. of water for 8 mins.
4. Then top your couscous with the pineapple mix.
5. Enjoy.

QUINOA
Forever

🥣 Prep Time: 30 mins
🕒 Total Time: 1 hr 25 mins

Servings per Recipe: 8
Calories   195 kcal
Fat   9.8 g
Carbohydrates   22.1g
Protein   6.3 g
Cholesterol   18 mg
Sodium   197 mg

Ingredients

1 C. quinoa
1 tbsp butter
2 C. chicken broth
1/2 C. diced green bell pepper
1/2 C. diced red onion
1 C. corn
1 (15 oz.) can black beans, drained
1/4 C. chopped cilantro
1 large tomato, diced

1/2 C. fresh lime juice, or to taste
2 tbsps balsamic vinegar
2 tbsps olive oil
1 tbsp adobo seasoning
1/2 C. feta cheese
salt and black pepper to taste

Directions

1. Get a bowl, combine: cheese, green peppers, adobo, onions, olive oil, corn, vinegar, black beans, lime, cilantro, and tomatoes.
2. Run cold water over your quinoa until it runs clear. Then toast the quinoa in butter for 4 mins.
3. Add in the broth and get it boiling.
4. Once everything is boiling, set the heat to low, and cook for 12 mins.
5. After the quinoa has cooked, add the cheese mix and also some pepper and salt.
6. Place everything in a bowl, in the fridge, for 40 mins.
7. Enjoy.

Green Beans and Black Beans Couscous

Prep Time: 25 mins
Total Time: 1 hr

Servings per Recipe: 6
Calories	262 kcal
Fat	2.2 g
Carbohydrates	52.2g
Protein	10.2 g
Cholesterol	0 mg
Sodium	843 mg

Ingredients

2 tsps vegetable oil
1 medium onion, chopped
2 cloves garlic, minced
1 1/2 lbs butternut squash, peeled and cut into bite-size pieces
1 (14.5 oz.) can diced tomatoes with chilies
1 (14.5 oz.) can vegetable broth
1/2 C. water
1 tsp ground cumin
1 tsp dried oregano
1/4 tsp black pepper
1 (14.5 oz.) can Green Beans, undrained
1 (15 oz.) can black beans, rinsed and drained
Hot cooked couscous
Chopped fresh cilantro (optional)

Directions

1. Stir fry your garlic and onion for 7 mins in oil. Then add in: black pepper, squash, oregano, diced tomatoes, cumin, water, and broth.
2. Get everything boiling for 2 mins, then lower the heat and let the veggies gently boil for 32 mins covered with a lid.
3. After 32 mins add both of the beans and cook for 7 more mins.
4. Add some cilantro as a garnish.
5. Enjoy.

DELUXE
Fish Tacos

Prep Time: 40mins
Total Time: 45 mins

Servings per Recipe: 8
Calories 409 kcal
Fat 18.8 g
Carbohydrates 43g
Protein 17.3 g
Cholesterol 54 mg
Sodium 407 mg

Ingredients

1 C. all-purpose flour
2 tbsps cornstarch
1 tsp baking powder
1/2 tsp salt
1 egg
1 C. apple juice
1/2 C. plain yogurt
1/2 C. mayonnaise
1 lime, juiced
1 jalapeno pepper, minced
1 tsp minced capers
1/2 tsp dried oregano

1/2 tsp ground cumin
1/2 tsp dried dill weed
1 tsp ground cayenne pepper
1 quart oil for frying
1 lb cod fillets, cut into 2 to 3 oz. portions
1 (12 oz.) package corn tortillas
1/2 medium head cabbage, finely shredded

Directions

1. Add oil to a big frying pot or deep fryer and get it to 375 degrees.
2. Blend the following in your blender until smooth: apple juice and eggs. Put everything into a bowl.
3. Get a 2nd bowl, evenly mix: salt, flour, baking powder, and cornstarch.
4. Combine both bowls and stir to get an even batter.
5. Get a 3rd bowl, mix: mayo, lime juice, cayenne, jalapenos, dill, capers, cumin, yogurt, and oregano.
6. Coat your fish with some flour and enter it into the batter. Fry until crispy then remove excess oil with some paper towels. Then fry the tortillas.
7. Layer some fish, then some cabbage, and finally some mayo sauce on each tortilla.
8. Enjoy.

Lime Beef Tacos

Prep Time: 15 mins
Total Time: 25 mins

Servings per Recipe: 9
Calories	379 kcal
Fat	21.4 g
Carbohydrates	28.1g
Protein	20.3 g
Cholesterol	58 mg
Sodium	69 mg

Ingredients

2 lbs top sirloin steak, cut into thin strips
salt and ground black pepper to taste
1/4 C. vegetable oil
18 (6 inch) corn tortillas
1 onion, diced
4 fresh jalapeno peppers, seeded and chopped
1 bunch fresh cilantro, chopped
4 limes, cut into wedges

Directions

1. Stir fry your steak for 6 mins. Then coat it with some pepper and salt. Set it aside.
2. Add more oil to the pan and fry your tortillas.
3. Layer cilantro, steak, jalapenos, and onions on each fried tortilla and then garnish with some lime.
4. Enjoy.

VEGETARIAN
Swiss Tacos

Prep Time: 20 mins
Total Time: 1 hr 5 mins

Servings per Recipe: 4
Calories   354 kcal
Fat   13 g
Carbohydrates   48.8g
Protein   14.4 g
Cholesterol   20 mg
Sodium   531 mg

Ingredients

1 1/2 tbsps olive oil
1 large onion, cut into 1/4-inch slices
3 cloves garlic, minced
1 tbsp red pepper flakes, or to taste
1/2 C. chicken broth
1 bunch Swiss chard, tough stems removed and leaves cut crosswise into 1 1/2-inch slices
1 pinch salt
12 corn tortillas
1 C. crumbled queso fresco cheese
3/4 C. salsa

Directions

1. Stir fry your onions for 11 mins and then combine in some red pepper flakes, and garlic and cook for another 2 mins.
2. Add into the onions: salt, chicken broth, and Swiss chard.
3. Place a lid on the pan and set the heat to low. Simmer for 7 mins.
4. Take off the lid and raise the heat a bit. Stir the contents for 6 mins until no liquid remains.
5. Shut off the heat fully.
6. Get a 2nd pan and toast the tortillas for 2 mins each side with a low level of heat.
7. Layer queso fresco cheese, chard mix, and salsa on each tortilla.
8. Enjoy.

Avocado Tacos Supreme

Prep Time: 15 mins
Total Time: 20 mins

Servings per Recipe: 6
Calories	455 kcal
Fat	21.1 g
Carbohydrates	70.1g
Protein	13.8 g
Cholesterol	0 mg
Sodium	604 mg

Ingredients

- 1 (14.5 oz.) can whole tomatoes, drained, rinsed, patted dry
- 2 roma tomatoes, quartered
- 1 onion, chopped, divided
- 1 clove garlic, coarsely chopped
- 1/4 C. fresh cilantro
- 1/2 jalapeno pepper
- salt and pepper to taste
- 4 avocados, halved with pits removed
- 12 (6 inch) whole wheat tortillas
- 1 (15 oz.) can kidney beans, rinsed and drained
- 2 C. torn romaine lettuce

Directions

1. Set your oven to 350 degrees before doing anything else.
2. Enter the following into a blender or processor: jalapenos, fresh and canned tomatoes, garlic, and half of your onions.
3. Process or pulse a few times. Do not make a smooth mix. Only dice the contents a bit.
4. Get a bowl, mix until smooth: pepper, the rest of the onions, salt, and avocados.
5. Get a casserole dish and cook your tortillas in the oven for 5 mins.
6. Layer on each tortilla: lettuce, guacamole, salsa, and beans.
7. Enjoy.

COLESLAW
Tacos

🥣 Prep Time: 20 mins
🕐 Total Time: 20 mins

Servings per Recipe: 6
Calories   27 kcal
Fat   0.1 g
Carbohydrates   6.6 g
Protein   1.1 g
Cholesterol   0 mg
Sodium   19 mg

Ingredients

1/2 small head cabbage, chopped
1 jalapeno pepper, seeded and minced
1/2 red onion, minced
1 carrot, chopped
1 tbsp chopped fresh cilantro
1 lime, juiced

Directions

1. Simply combine all the ingredients in a bowl.
2. Enjoy on warm tortillas with your choice of meat and salsa.

Arizona
Tacos

Prep Time: 15 mins
Total Time: 45 mins

Servings per Recipe: 8
Calories   520 kcal
Fat   30.7 g
Carbohydrates   32.6 g
Protein   26.7 g
Cholesterol   96 mg
Sodium   1289 mg

Ingredients

- 1 onion, chopped
- 2 (15 oz.) cans ranch-style beans
- 1 (15.25 oz.) can whole kernel corn
- 1 (10 oz.) can diced tomatoes with green chile peppers
- 1 (14.5 oz.) can peeled and diced tomatoes with juice
- 1 (1.25 oz.) package taco seasoning mix

Directions

1. Cook your onions and beef for 10 mins then remove oil excesses.
2. Combine with the beef your chili peppers, beans, taco seasoning, tomatoes, and corn. Stir the contents for a min. Cook over medium heat for 17 mins.
3. Enjoy.

SHRIMP
Tacos

Prep Time: 15 mins
Total Time: 47 mins

Servings per Recipe: 4
Calories 567 kcal
Fat 23.1 g
Carbohydrates 59.5g
Protein 31.2 g
Cholesterol 188 mg
Sodium 951 mg

Ingredients

1 mango - peeled, seeded and diced
1 ripe avocado - peeled, pitted, and diced
2 tomatoes, diced
1/2 C. chopped fresh cilantro
1/4 C. chopped red onion
3 cloves garlic, minced
1/2 tsp salt
2 tbsps lime juice
1/4 C. honey butter
1 lb salad shrimp
4 (10 inch) flour tortillas, warmed

Directions

1. Get bowl combine: lime juice, mango, salt, avocadoes, garlic, onions, and cilantro. Place a lid or some plastic wrap on the bowl.
2. Put the bowl in the fridge for 40 mins.
3. Stir fry your shrimp for 4 mins in the honey butter.
4. Layer on your tortillas: mango mix, and shrimp.
5. Enjoy.

Teriyaki Tacos

Prep Time: 30 mins
Total Time: 40 mins

Servings per Recipe: 2
Calories	465 kcal
Fat	15 g
Carbohydrates	69.7g
Protein	33.2 g
Cholesterol	49 mg
Sodium	3853 mg

Ingredients

- 4 Mission(R) Soft Taco Flour Tortillas
- 8 oz. sirloin steak, chopped into 1x1/4-inch pieces
- 1/2 C. teriyaki marinade
- 1/2 C. cucumber, grated
- 1/2 C. carrots, shredded
- 1/2 tsp fresh ginger, grated
- 1/2 tsp black sesame seeds
- 1 tbsp fresh orange juice
- 1/2 tsp soy sauce
- 1/2 tsp honey
- Salt and pepper to taste
- 1/2 C. sliced green onions

Directions

1. Get a bowl, mix: teriyaki and steak.
2. Place a lid on the container and put it in the fridge for 30 mins.
3. Get a 2nd bowl, combine: honey, pepper, cucumbers, ginger, soy sauce, carrots, sesame seeds, salt, and orange juice.
4. Put this in the fridge as well with a covering until you are ready to assemble your tacos.
5. Stir fry your steak and marinade for 12 mins.
6. Layer the following on each tortillas: sliced green onions, one fourth C. of carrot mix, and an even amount of steak.

CILANTRO
BBQ Corn

⏲ Prep Time: 15 mins
🕐 Total Time: 1 hr 35 mins

Servings per Recipe: 8
Calories   282 kcal
Fat   24.1 g
Carbohydrates   17.4g
Protein   3.2 g
Cholesterol   61 mg
Sodium   188 mg

Ingredients

1 cup butter
1/4 cup chopped fresh cilantro
1 1/2 tablespoons fresh lime juice
1 pinch cayenne pepper
8 ears corn on the cob, husked pealed to the bottom, corn silk removed

3 quarts cold water, or as needed to cover

Directions

1. Get a bowl and begin to whisk your butter in it until the butter is soft and creamy then combine in the cayenne, lime juice, and cilantro. Place a covering of plastic on the bowl and put everything in the fridge until it is cold.
2. Once your corn has all the silk remove close the husk back over the ears and submerge everything in water in a big bowl for 30 mins.
3. Now get your grill outside hot and coat the grate with oil.
4. Begin to grill your corn for 23 to 26 mins flipping the ears constantly. Chill the husks completely then remove then once 23 mins has elapsed.
5. Coat your corn with the butter mix.
6. Enjoy.

Tostadas

Prep Time: 20 mins
Total Time: 20 mins

Servings per Recipe: 8
Calories	252 kcal
Fat	11.3 g
Carbohydrates	27g
Protein	12.1 g
Cholesterol	34 mg
Sodium	945 mg

Ingredients

- 8 (6 inch) Old El Paso(R) Flour Tortillas for Soft Tacos & Fajitas
- 1 (11 ounce) can Green Giant(R) Steam Crisp(R) Mexicorn(R) whole kernel corn with red and green peppers, drained
- 1 1/2 cups shredded cooked chicken
- 1 (16 ounce) jar Old El Paso(R) Salsa (any variety)
- 1/2 cup sour cream
- 1 tablespoon milk, or as needed
- 2 1/2 cups shredded lettuce
- 1 cup shredded Cheddar or Monterey Jack cheese
- 1/4 cup sliced green onions

Directions

1. Set your oven to 375 degrees before doing anything else.
2. Lay your tortillas in a casserole dish and cook them in the oven for 11 mins.
3. At the same time add your salsa, chicken, and corn to pot and let it cook for 4 mins with a high level of heat while stirring.
4. Get a bowl, combine: milk and sour cream.
5. Once your tortillas are done baking cover them with the chicken mix and some lettuce then cheese. Top everything with the milk mix then green onions.
6. Enjoy.

THURSDAY'S
Quesadilla's

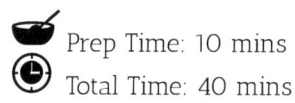

Prep Time: 10 mins
Total Time: 40 mins

Servings per Recipe: 8
Calories	363 kcal
Fat	14.5 g
Carbohydrates	45.6 g
Protein	13.9 g
Cholesterol	26 mg
Sodium	732 mg

Ingredients

- 2 teaspoons olive oil
- 3 tablespoons finely chopped onion
- 1 (15.5 ounce) can black beans, drained and rinsed
- 1 (10 ounce) can whole kernel corn, drained
- 1 tablespoon brown sugar
- 1/4 cup salsa
- 1/4 teaspoon red pepper flakes
- 2 tablespoons butter, divided
- 8 (8 inch) flour tortillas
- 1 1/2 cups shredded Monterey Jack cheese, divided

Directions

1. Begin to stir fry your onion in oil for 3 mins then combine in the corn and beans and stir everything. Now add your pepper flakes, sugar, and salsa. Stir everything again and let the mix cook for 4 mins.
2. Get 2 tbsps of butter hot in a frying pan then once it is add in your tortilla to the butter. Cover the tortilla with cheese and some of the corn mix.
3. Place another tortilla over the bean mix and let it cook for a few minx then flip it and cook it for 2 more mins. Add some more butter and continue making quesadilla in this manner until all the ingredients have been used up.
4. Enjoy.

Aztec Corn Bread

Prep Time: 30 mins
Total Time: 55 mins

Servings per Recipe: 9
Calories   220 kcal
Fat   8.8 g
Carbohydrates   29.3g
Protein   6 g
Cholesterol   61 mg
Sodium   422 mg

Ingredients

4 slices turkey bacon
5 tablespoons maple syrup, divided, plus additional for serving (optional)
1 cup yellow cornmeal
3/4 cup all-purpose flour
2 1/2 teaspoons baking powder
1/2 teaspoon salt
1 cup milk
2 eggs
1/4 cup butter, melted

Directions

1. Set your oven to 400 degrees before doing anything else.
2. Place your pieces of bacon into a baking dish and cook them in the oven for 10 mins. Add in 1 tbsp of maple syrup over the bacon evenly then let the pieces cook for 3 more mins. Once the pieces have cooled off chopped them.
3. Get a bowl, combine: salt, cornmeal, baking powder, and flour.
4. Get a 2nd bowl, combine butter, the rest of the maple syrup (4 tbsps), eggs, and milk. Whisk this mix together completely then combine both bowls evenly.
5. Stir in the bacon then combine everything.
6. Pour the entire mix into a casserole dish and cook everything for 22 mins.
7. Top the corn bread with some more honey if you like.
8. Enjoy.

CHICAGO
Hot Dogs

Prep Time: 15 mins
Total Time: 25 mins

Servings per Recipe: 4
Calories 298.9
Fat 14.6g
Cholesterol 22.5mg
Sodium 888.1mg
Carbohydrates 31.8g
Protein 10.8g

Ingredients

4 natural casing beef frankfurters
4 hot dog buns
1 small onion, diced fine
3 - 4 tsp sweet pickle relish
1 cold-pack kosher dill pickle, quartered lengthwise
1 small tomatoes, sliced into julienne strips
4 - 8 pickled sport bell peppers
brown mustard, with horseradish, to taste
celery seed
poppy seed
water, for simmering

Directions

1. In a pan, add water and frankfurters and simmer for about 10 minutes.
2. In a microwave safe plate, place the buns and microwave till slightly warm and soft.
3. Arrange 1 frankfurter in each bun and top with the mustard, followed by dill spear, relish, onion, tomato and 1-2 sport peppers.
4. Serve with a sprinkling of the celery and poppy seeds.

Simple Spring Lunch Hot Dogs

Prep Time: 15 mins
Total Time: 30 mins

Servings per Recipe: 2
Calories   328.5
Fat   18.4g
Cholesterol   32.9mg
Sodium   905.6mg
Carbohydrates   28.3g
Protein   11.6g

Ingredients

2 kosher hot dogs
4 slices bread
2 slices American cheese
ketchup, to taste
other condiments, to taste

Directions

1. Prepare the hot dogs according to package's
2. Meanwhile in a toaster, toast the bread.
3. Spread the ketchup over the 2 pieced of the bread evenly.
4. Arrange 1 cheese slice over the over remaining bread slices.
5. Now, slice them down the center lengthwise, and then again horizontally.
6. Arrange the hot dog on the bread slices with the cheese.
7. Add the condiments of your choice.
8. Top with the slices of bread with ketchup.

SAUCY
Spanish Mussels

Prep Time: 15 mins
Total Time: 27 mins

Servings per Recipe: 4
Calories   510.3
Fat   13.9 g
Cholesterol   127.3 mg
Sodium   1315.3 mg
Carbohydrates   27.3 g
Protein   55.9 g

Ingredients

1 tbsp olive oil
1 large onion, chopped
1 tbsp minced garlic
1 (16 oz.) cans diced tomatoes
1/2 C. minced parsley
pepper

1 C. chicken broth
4 lbs cleaned mussels

Directions

1. In a large pan, heat the oil and sauté the onion and garlic for about 5 minutes.
2. Stir in the parsley, tomatoes and black pepper and cook for about 2 minutes.
3. Stir in the broth and cook for about 2 minutes.
4. Add the mussels and simmer, covered for about 3-4 minutes, stirring occasionally.
5. Discard any unopened mussels.
6. Serve with a topping of the French crusty bread.

Mussels Martinique

Prep Time: 15 mins
Total Time: 30 mins

Servings per Recipe: 2
Calories   740.7
Fat   55.0g
Cholesterol   175.5mg
Sodium   1167.3mg
Carbohydrates   23.0g
Protein   37.7g

Ingredients

4 C. mussels
2 tbsp extra virgin olive oil
2 tbsp yellow onions, chopped
2 tbsp garlic, chopped
2 tbsp Pernod
1 tbsp fresh basil, chopped
1/2 lemon, juice and pulp of
Lemon Butter Sauce (use 3/4 C.)
1/4 C. real butter
2 tbsp yellow onions, minced
2 tbsp garlic, minced

1/3 C. fresh lemon juice
2 tbsp water
kosher salt
white pepper, to taste
2 tbsp cold butter

Directions

1. For lemon butter sauce in a frying pan, melt the butter on low heat.
2. Remove from the heat and keep aside till the milk solids settle to the bottom.
3. Discard the milk solids.
4. In a skillet, heat the 2 tbsp of the clarified butter and sauté the onion and garlic till tender.
5. Stir in the salt, black pepper, water and lemon juice and simmer for about 2-3 minutes.
6. Remove from the heat and stir in the cold butter.
7. Meanwhile in a bowl of cold water, soak the mussels for about 8 minutes.
8. With a sharp knife, remove the beards and rinse under cold water.
9. In a skillet, heat the oil and cook the mussels, covered for about 2-6 minutes.
10. Stir in the onion and garlic and cook, covered for about 1 minute.
11. Stir in the lemon butter, Pernod, basil and lemon juice and cook for about 45 seconds.
12. Discard any unopened mussels.
13. Serve immediately.

MUSSELS
Toscano

🥣 Prep Time: 15 mins
🕐 Total Time: 15 mins

Servings per Recipe: 2
Calories   614.5
Fat   23.2g
Cholesterol   173.7mg
Sodium   1558.8mg
Carbohydrates   25.5g
Protein   62.3g

Ingredients

2 1/4 lbs mussels, cleaned
1/2 C. chicken broth
2 green onions, chopped
2 - 3 garlic cloves, minced
1/4 C. fresh dill, chopped plus extra to garnish

1/4 C. fresh parsley
1/4 tsp dried red chili pepper
2 ripe plum tomatoes, chopped
2 tbsp butter

Directions

1. In a large pan, add the mussels and broth on high heat and bring to a boil.
2. Cook, covered for a few minutes, stirring continuously.
3. Stir in the remaining ingredients except the butter and cook, covered for about 3-4 minutes on medium-high heat.
4. Stir in the butter and remove from the heat.
5. Serve with a garnishing of the dill.

Creamy Dijon Mussels

Prep Time: 10 mins
Total Time: 25 mins

Servings per Recipe: 4
Calories	473.5
Fat	24.6g
Cholesterol	151.5mg
Sodium	1114.4mg
Carbohydrates	16.6g
Protein	41.8g

Ingredients

- 2 - 3 tbsp butter
- 1/4 C. finely chopped onion
- 2 tbsp finely chopped shallots
- 1 tsp finely chopped garlic
- 3 lbs mussels, beards removed, cleaned and scrubbed
- sea salt
- fresh ground pepper
- 1 bay leaf
- 2 sprigs fresh thyme
- 1/4 C. chicken broth
- 1/2 C. heavy cream
- 2 tbsp Dijon mustard
- 2 tbsp finely chopped flat leaf parsley

Directions

1. In a large pan, melt the butter and sauté the shallots onions and garlic till soft.
2. Stir in the remaining ingredients except the mustard and thyme and bring to a boil.
3. Reduce the heat to medium and simmer, covered for about 5 minutes, shaking the pan occasionally.
4. With a slotted spoon, transfer the mussels into a bowl and discard any unopened mussels.
5. Cover with a foil paper to keep them warm.
6. Cook the sauce for about 1 minute and discard the thyme and bay leaf. Add the mustard, beating continuously till heated completely.
7. Pour the sauce over the mussels and serve with a garnishing of the parsley alongside the crusty bread.

TOPPED
Mussel Platter

Prep Time: 15 mins
Total Time: 45 mins

Servings per Recipe: 2
Calories 732.2
Fat 24.0g
Cholesterol 127.3mg
Sodium 2481.1mg
Carbohydrates 38.4g
Protein 56.7g

Ingredients

1 C. onion (diced)
2 tbsp extra virgin olive oil
4 tbsp garlic (minced)
1/2 tsp red pepper flakes
1 bay leaf
1 tsp salt
1 tsp black pepper
4 oz. tomatoes (diced)
1 tsp basil
1 1/2 C. chicken broth
2 lbs mussels

Directions

1. In a large bowl of cold water, add the mussels and 2 tbsp of the flour.
2. Keep aside for about 10-15 minutes, then rinse under the cold water.
3. In a large skillet, heat the oil and sauté the onion,, garlic, bay leaf and red pepper flakes for about 6-10 minutes.
4. Stir in the tomatoes, basil, salt and black pepper and cook for about 3 minutes.
5. Add mussels and broth cook till all the mussels have opened.
6. Serve alongside the crusty bread.

Country Style Mussels with Leeks

Prep Time: 25 mins
Total Time: 40 mins

Servings per Recipe: 4
Calories   528.1
Fat   30.1g
Cholesterol   135.6mg
Sodium   892.3mg
Carbohydrates   22.5g
Protein   35.7g

Ingredients

3 medium leeks, cleaned and roughly chopped
3 garlic cloves, finely diced
2 tbsp olive oil
2 tbsp butter
3 oz. fish broth
1/4 pint heavy cream
2 1/2 lbs mussels, cleaned
1/4 C. parsley, roughly chopped

Directions

1. In a large pan, heat the oil and butter and sauté the garlic and leeks for about 5 minutes.
2. Stir in the broth and increase the heat and cook for about 1 minute.
3. Stir in the cream and bring to a boil.
4. Add the mussels and cook, covered till all the mussels have opened.
5. Discard any unopened mussels.
6. Serve alongside crusty bread.

MUSSELS
Marrakesh

🥣 Prep Time: 15 mins
🕐 Total Time: 45 mins

Servings per Recipe: 4
Calories 590.5
Fat 19.6g
Cholesterol 95.5mg
Sodium 1728.0mg
Carbohydrates 55.7g
Protein 48.0g

Ingredients

1 medium onion, coarsely chopped
2 garlic cloves, thinly sliced
1 1/4 tsp ground cumin
1 tsp paprika
1 tsp ground ginger
3/8 tsp ground cinnamon
1/8 tsp cayenne
3 tbsp olive oil
1 tbsp cider vinegar
1 (15 oz.) cans chickpeas, drained and rinsed
2 tsp sugar
1 (28 oz.) cans whole tomatoes with juice, juice reserved and tomatoes coarsely chopped
3 lbs mussels, scrubbed and beards removed
2 tbsp fresh flat-leaf parsley, chopped

Directions

1. In a large heavy pan, heat the oil on medium-low heat and sauté the onion and garlic for about 6 minutes.
2. Add the vinegar and simmer for about 1 minute.
3. Stir in the sugar, chickpeas, tomatoes and reserved juice and increase the heat to medium.
4. Simmer, stirring occasionally for about 15 minutes.
5. Add the mussels and simmer, covered for about 3-6 minutes.
6. Discard any unopened mussels.
7. Stir in the parsley and serve.

Florida Mussel Soup

 Prep Time: 15 mins
 Total Time: 35 mins

Servings per Recipe: 4
Calories	241.9
Fat	9.6g
Cholesterol	33.6mg
Sodium	566.5mg
Carbohydrates	15.9g
Protein	15.5g

Ingredients

- 30 fresh mussels (scrub and debeard)
- 2 garlic cloves, crushed
- 1 onion, peeled and chopped
- 2 tbsp olive oil
- 2 tbsp parsley, chopped
- 1 tsp chopped fresh chili pepper
- 2 tbsp lemon juice
- 3/4 C. fish broth
- 1 1/2 C. water
- 400 g crushed tomatoes with juice
- salt and black pepper

Directions

1. In a large pan, heat the oil and sauté the onion and garlic till tender.
2. Stir in the chili pepper and parsley and sauté for about 1-2 minutes.
3. Add the water, broth and lemon juice and increase the heat.
4. Bring to a boil and reduce the heat to medium.
5. Simmer, covered for about 5 minutes.
6. Discard any unopened mussels.
7. Discard the top shell from each mussel.
8. Season with the salt and black pepper and remove from the heat.

CREAMY
City Mussels

🥣 Prep Time: 15 mins
🕐 Total Time: 35 mins

Servings per Recipe: 2
Calories 1667.2
Fat 99.6g1
Cholesterol 509.2mg
Sodium 2917.5mg
Carbohydrates 65.3g
Protein 115.1g

Ingredients

6 tbsp butter
4 garlic cloves, minced
4 shallots, minced
1/4 C. parsley, chopped
6 tbsp lemon juice
3 tomatoes, seeded and diced small
4 lbs mussels
3/4 C. fish broth

1 C. heavy whipping cream
1 lemon, zested and cut into slices
Garnish
chopped parsley

Directions

1. In a bowl, mix together the shallot, garlic, 1 tbsp of the parsley, 1/4 C. of the lemon juice, butter, salt and black pepper.
2. In a Dutch oven, melt the butter on medium heat and sauté till shallots become tender.
3. Add the mussels and stir for about 1 minute.
4. Stir in the 3/4 C. of the cream, broth, lemon peel, salt and black pepper.
5. Place the tomato and lemon slices on top and simmer, covered for about 8-10 minutes.
6. With a slotted spoon, transfer the mussels into a bowl and discard any unopened mussels.
7. Cook the sauce for about 5 minutes.
8. Add the parsley and remaining lemon juice and cream.
9. Boil for about 1 minute and pour over the mussels.
10. Serve immediately.

Cajun Style Tilapia I

Prep Time: 10 mins
Total Time: 30 mins

Servings per Recipe: 4
Calories	284 kcal
Fat	18.6 g
Carbohydrates	5.7g
Protein	24.5 g
Cholesterol	59 mg
Sodium	501 mg

Ingredients

- 4 (4 oz.) fillets tilapia
- salt and pepper to taste
- 1 tbsp Cajun seasoning, or to taste
- 1 tbsp cilantro
- 1 lemon, thinly sliced
- 1/4 C. mayonnaise
- 1/2 C. sour cream
- 1/8 tsp garlic powder
- 1 tsp fresh lemon juice
- 2 tbsps diced fresh dill

Directions

1. Coat a casserole dish with nonstick spray and set your oven to 350 degrees before doing anything else.
2. Top your pieces of fish with: Cajun seasoning, pepper, cilantro, and salt. Then place them in the casserole dish.
3. Garnish each piece of fish with some lemon and cook everything in the oven for 17 mins.
4. Now get a bowl, combine: dill, mayo, lemon juice, sour cream, and garlic powder.
5. When serving your tilapia garnish it with the mayo mix.
6. Enjoy.

EASY
Veggie Baked Tilapia

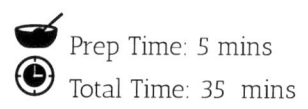

Prep Time: 5 mins
Total Time: 35 mins

Servings per Recipe: 4
Calories   172 kcal
Fat   3.6 g
Carbohydrates   7.3g
Protein   24.8 g
Cholesterol   46 mg
Sodium   354 mg

Ingredients

4 (4 oz.) fillets tilapia
2 tsps butter
1/4 tsp Old Bay Seasoning TM, or to taste
1/2 tsp garlic salt, or to taste

1 lemon, sliced
1 (16 oz.) package frozen cauliflower with broccoli and red pepper

Directions

1. Coat a casserole dish with nonstick spray and then set your oven to 375 degrees before doing anything else.
2. Layer your pieces of fish in the casserole dish and top them with the garlic salt, pepper, regular salt, and old bay seasoning before adding some butter to each.
3. Pour your veggies around the fish and place a covering of foil around the dish.
4. Cook everything in the oven for 27 mins.
5. Enjoy.

Raspberries and Dijon Tilapia

Prep Time: 10 mins
Total Time: 20 mins

Servings per Recipe: 4
Calories	205 kcal
Fat	10.2 g
Carbohydrates	3.9 g
Protein	23.5 g
Cholesterol	65 mg
Sodium	241 mg

Ingredients

- 2 tbsps butter
- 3 tsps lemon juice, divided
- 1 tbsp melted butter
- 1 tsp Dijon mustard
- 1 tsp raspberry vinegar
- 2 tsps honey
- 1 tsp diced fresh tarragon
- salt and pepper to taste
- 1 lb tilapia fillets

Directions

1. Cover a broiler pan with foil and two tbsp of butter then turn on the broiler of your oven to low if possible.
2. Get a bowl, mix: pepper, lemon juice (1 tsp), salt, melted butter, tarragon, mustard, honey, and vinegar.
3. Layer your pieces of fish in the casserole dish and cook them under the broiler for 3 mins per side then remove them from the oven and top them with half of the honey mix.
4. Cook the contents for 2 more mins.
5. Finally garnish the fish with the rest of the honey mix.
6. Enjoy.

TERIYAKI
Chicken Stir Fry with Noodles

Prep Time: 15 mins
Total Time: 35 mins

Servings per Recipe: 4
Calories   445 kcal
Fat   11.4 g
Carbohydrates   60.6g
Protein   18 g
Cholesterol   33 mg
Sodium   1415 mg

Ingredients

1 large skinless, boneless chicken breast, cut in bite-sized pieces
1 pinch garlic powder, or to taste
1 pinch onion powder, or to taste
freshly ground black pepper to taste
1 (8 oz) package dried rice noodles
4 C. hot water, or as needed
3 tbsp vegetable oil, divided
4 cloves garlic, minced
1 onion, chopped

1 green bell pepper, chopped
1/2 C. fish broth, or to taste
1/4 C. soy sauce, or to taste
2 tbsp teriyaki sauce, or to taste
1 (6 oz) can sweet baby corn, drained
3 green onions, chopped

Directions

1. Season the chicken with garlic powder, onion powder, and black pepper.
2. Fill a large bowl with hot water. Place in it the noodles and let the soak for 12 min. Remove it from the water and slice it in half.
3. Place a large pan over medium heat. Heat 1 1/2 tbsp of oil in it. Add the garlic and cook it for 1 min 30 sec.
4. Stir in the bell pepper with onion and cook them for 6 min while stirring all the time. Stir in the remaining oil.
5. Add the chicken and cook them for 8 min while stirring them often. Add the broth, soy sauce, and teriyaki sauce. Cook the stir fry for 4 min.
6. Stir in the baby corn and green onions with rice and noodles. Cook them for 4 min.
7. Serve your stir fry warm.
8. Enjoy.

Tangerine Chicken Stir Fry

- Prep Time: 20 mins
- Total Time: 55 mins

Servings per Recipe: 6
Calories	467 kcal
Fat	29.2 g
Carbohydrates	17.1g
Protein	34.8 g
Cholesterol	108 mg
Sodium	552 mg

Ingredients

- 1/2 onion, minced
- 1/2 C. water
- 1/2 C. tangerine juice
- 1/3 C. coconut aminos
- 1/3 C. coconut oil
- 4 green onions, sliced into rounds
- 2 cloves garlic, minced
- 1 (1 inch) piece fresh ginger, minced
- 1 tsp vinegar
- salt and ground black pepper to taste
- 2 lb boneless chicken breast, cut into cubes
- 1 C. string beans, trimmed, or to taste
- 1 C. chopped broccoli
- 1/4 C. ghee
- 1 (8 oz) package fresh mushrooms, sliced
- 1/2 onion, sliced
- 2 tbsp coconut oil
- 3 zucchini, spiralized
- 2 carrots, shredded

Directions

1. Get a mixing bowl: Mix in it the onion, water, tangerine juice, coconut aminos, 1/3 C. coconut oil, green onions, garlic, ginger, vinegar, salt, and black pepper to make the marinade.
2. Get a large mixing bowl: Toss in it half of the marinade with chicken.
3. Fill a large pot with water and a pinch of salt. Cook it until it starts boiling. Cook in it the string beans and broccoli for 2 min.
4. Remove them from the hot water and place them in a ice bath right away to cool down. Remove them from the water and place them aside.
5. Place a large pan or wok over medium heat. Melt the ghee in it. Add the mushroom and cook it for 8 min. Drain it and add it to the broccoli and bean mix.
6. Add the onion into the same skillet and cook it for 8 min. Drain it and add it to the broccoli mix.
7. Drain the chicken and reserve the marinade.

8. Place a large skillet over medium heat and grease it with some oil. Cook in it the chicken for 12 min while stirring them often.
9. Transfer the cooked chicken to the broccoli mix.
10. Place a large pan over medium heat. Heat 2 tbsp of coconut oil in it. Cook in it the carrot with zucchini for 4 min.
11. Stir in the remaining half of the marinade with the reserved chicken marinade and the broccoli mix. Cook them for 8 min while stirring them often.
12. Serve your stir fry chicken warm.
13. Enjoy.

Basmati

Chicken Stir Fry Spears

🥣 Prep Time: 20 mins
🕐 Total Time: 1 hr 10 mins

Servings per Recipe: 4
Calories   1095 kcal
Fat   47.7 g
Carbohydrates   86.7g
Protein   77.8 g
Cholesterol   270 mg
Sodium   610 mg

Ingredients

- 2 C. basmati rice
- 4 C. water
- 1 tbsp vegetable oil
- 1 red onion, cut into 1/2-inch slices
- 3 1/2 lb skinless, boneless chicken thighs, cut into 2-inch strips
- 1 tbsp minced fresh ginger root
- 6 cloves garlic, minced
- 3 C. crimini mushrooms, cut in half
- 12 fresh asparagus, trimmed and cut into 2-inch pieces
- 2 small red bell peppers, cut into 1/2-inch strips
- 1 tbsp fish sauce
- 1 egg
- 2 C. fresh basil leaves
- 1 C. fresh cilantro leaves, chopped
- 2 tbsp sesame seeds, for garnish
- tamari soy sauce to taste

Directions

1. Cook the rice according to the directions on the package.
2. Place a large wok or pan over medium heat. Heat the oil in it. Add the onion and cook it for 4 min.
3. Stir in the chicken with ginger and garlic. Cook them for 8 min. Stir in the mushrooms, asparagus, bell peppers, and fish sauce. Cook them for 7 min.
4. Stir in the basil and cook them for 1 min. Serve your stir fry right away with the white rice.
5. Enjoy.

GRILLED CHICKEN
Stir Fry Linguine

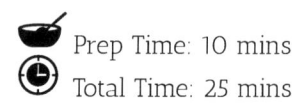

Prep Time: 10 mins
Total Time: 25 mins

Servings per Recipe: 6
Calories 559 kcal
Fat 12.7 g
Carbohydrates 66.3g
Protein 43.6 g
Cholesterol 88 mg
Sodium 335 mg

Ingredients

1 (22 oz) package Tyson(R) Grilled and Ready(R) Fully Cooked Frozen Grilled Chicken Breast Strips
2 C. sliced fresh mushrooms
2 tbsp vegetable oil
2 C. frozen sweet pepper stir-fry
2/3 C. stir-fry sauce

1 lb linguine, prepared according to package directions

Directions

1. Cook the chicken according to the instructions on the package.
2. Place a large wok or pan over medium heat. Heat the oil in it. Add the mushroom and cook it for 5 min.
3. Stir in the pepper and cook them for 3 min. Stir in the chicken with sauce and cook them for 4 min.
4. Serve your stir fry hot with the linguine.
5. Enjoy.

Beachy Chicken Stir Fry

Prep Time: 20 mins
Total Time: 42 mins

Servings per Recipe: 4
Calories   419 kcal
Fat   12.5 g
Carbohydrates   49.1g
Protein   30.4 g
Cholesterol   61 mg
Sodium   579 mg

Ingredients

- 14 oz skinless, boneless chicken breast, thinly sliced
- 1 egg white, beaten
- 2 tsp cornstarch
- 1 tsp sesame oil
- 1 (8 oz) package Chinese egg noodles
- 2 tbsp vegetable oil, or as needed
- 1/2 C. chicken broth
- 3 spring onions, chopped, or to taste
- 1 1/2 tbsp light soy sauce
- 1 tbsp apple cider
- 1/2 tsp ground white pepper
- 1/2 tsp ground black pepper
- 1 tbsp cornstarch
- 2 tsp water
- 2 tbsp oyster sauce
- 1 C. fresh bean sprouts, or to taste

Directions

1. Cook the noodles according to the instructions on the package. Place it aside.
2. Get a large mixing bowl: Mix in it the chicken with egg white, 2 tsp cornstarch, and sesame oil.
3. Place a large skillet over medium heat. Heat the oil in it. Cook in it the noodles until it becomes golden and slightly crisp for 4 min on each side. Remove it from the pan and place it aside.
4. Add the chicken to the skillet and cook it for 4 min. Drain and it and place it aside.
5. Stir the stock with spring onions, soy sauce, apple cider, white pepper, and black pepper into the same skillet.
6. Get a small mixing bowl: Whisk in it 1 tbsp cornstarch and water. Add the mix to the skillet with oyster sauce, chicken and bean sprouts.
7. Cook them until the mix becomes thick. Serve your stir fry with the noodles warm.
8. Enjoy.

FRIED TERIYAKI
Chicken Rice

Prep Time: 15 mins
Total Time: 23 mins

Servings per Recipe: 4
Calories	506 kcal
Fat	16.5 g
Carbohydrates	55.3g
Protein	32 g
Cholesterol	65 mg
Sodium	800 mg

Ingredients

1 lb skinless, boneless chicken breasts, cut into thin strips
1/4 C. teriyaki sauce, divided
3 tbsp vegetable oil, divided
3 scallions, thinly sliced
2 cloves garlic, minced
1 tbsp minced fresh ginger root
8 oz snow peas, trimmed
1/4 C. low-sodium chicken broth
4 C. cooked white rice
3 tbsp chopped roasted cashews

Directions

1. Get a large mixing bowl: Toss in it the chicken and 2 tbsp teriyaki sauce.
2. Place a large pan over medium heat. Heat 1 1/2 tbsp of oil in it. Cook in it the chicken for 6 min. Drain and place it aside.
3. Add the scallions, garlic, ginger, and remaining vegetable oil to the same pan. Cook them for 2 min. Add the broth with snow peas. Cook them for 4 min.
4. Add the rice, cooked chicken, and remaining teriyaki sauce. Cook them for 4 min. Fold in the cashews. Serve your stir fry warm.
5. Enjoy.

American Parsley Chicken Stir Fry

Prep Time: 10 mins
Total Time: 40 mins

Servings per Recipe: 6
Calories	425 kcal
Fat	9.4 g
Carbohydrates	61.2g
Protein	21.2 g
Cholesterol	44 mg
Sodium	786 mg

Ingredients

- 2 C. uncooked white rice
- 4 C. water
- 1 tbsp olive oil
- 1 tsp garlic salt
- 1 tsp black pepper
- 1 tsp dried parsley
- 3 skinless, boneless chicken breast halves, cut into strips
- 2 C. chopped broccoli
- 1 C. sliced carrots
- 1 C. sugar snap peas
- 1 (10.75 oz) can condensed cheddar cheese soup, such as Campbell's(R)
- 1/2 C. shredded Cheddar cheese

Directions

1. Cook the rice according to the directions on the package.
2. Place a large skillet over medium heat. Heat the oil in it. Add the garlic salt, black pepper, chicken and parsley. Cook them for 8 min.
3. Add the broccoli, carrots, and snap peas. Put on the lid and cook them for 7 min.
4. Add the condensed Cheddar cheese soup. Stir them well. Cook them until they start simmering while stirring them often.
5. Serve your stir fry hot with rice.
6. Enjoy.

SPICY CHICKEN
Noodles Stir Fry

Prep Time: 20 mins
Total Time: 35 mins

Servings per Recipe: 4
Calories   503 kcal
Fat   16.5 g
Carbohydrates   69.8g
Protein   26.5 g
Cholesterol   29 mg
Sodium   3868 mg

Ingredients

2 tbsp canola oil
1 tbsp sesame oil
2 skinless, boneless chicken breast halves - cut into bite-size pieces
2 cloves garlic, minced
2 tbsp Asian-style chile paste
1/2 C. soy sauce
1 tbsp canola oil
1/2 medium head cabbage, thinly sliced
1 onion, sliced
2 carrots, cut into matchsticks
1 tbsp salt
2 lb cooked yakisoba noodles
2 tbsp pickled ginger, or to taste (optional)

Directions

1. Place a large pan over medium heat. Heat 2 tbsp of canola oil and sesame oil in it. Cook in it the garlic with chicken for 2 min..
2. Add chili paste and cook them for 5 min. Stir in the soy sauce and cook them for 3 min. Transfer the chicken mix into a bowl and place it aside.
3. Heat 1 tbsp of canola oil in the same pan. Cook in it the cabbage, onion, carrots, and salt for 5 min.
4. Add back the chicken mix with noodles. Cook them for 5 min. Serve your stir fry hot.
5. Enjoy.

Spicy Chestnut Chicken Stir Fry

Prep Time: 30 mins
Total Time: 1 hr 30 mins

Servings per Recipe: 4
Calories 437 kcal
Fat 23.3 g
Carbohydrates 25.3g
Protein 34.4 g
Cholesterol 66 mg
Sodium 596 mg

Ingredients

1 lb skinless, boneless chicken breast halves - cut into chunks
2 tbsp water
2 tbsp soy sauce
2 tbsp sesame oil, divided
2 tbsp cornstarch, dissolved in 2 tbsp water
1 oz hot chile paste
1 tsp distilled white vinegar
2 tsp brown sugar
4 green onions, chopped
1 tbsp chopped garlic
1 (8 oz) can water chestnuts
4 oz chopped peanuts

Directions

1. Get a large mixing bowl: Whisk in it 1 tbsp water, 1 tbsp soy sauce, 1 tbsp oil, 1 tbsp cornstarch and water mix. Mix them well.
2. Add the chicken and stir them well. Place the mix in the fridge for 40 min.
3. Get a small mixing bowl: Stir in it 1 tbsp water, 1 tbsp soy sauce, 1 tbsp oil, 1 tbsp cornstarch and water mix, chili paste, vinegar and sugar.
4. Stir in the green onion, garlic, water chestnuts and peanuts to make the sauce.
5. Place a large skillet over medium heat. Cook in it the sauce for 2 min.
6. Place a another pan over medium heat. Grease it with some oil. Drain the chicken and cook it in the pan for 6 min.
7. Stir in the sauce into the chicken and cook them until the sauce becomes slightly thick. Serve your chicken stir fry warm.
8. Enjoy.

CARROT, CABBAGE, and Chicken Skillet

Prep Time: 20 mins
Total Time: 40 mins

Servings per Recipe: 6
Calories 369 kcal
Fat 4.9 g
Carbohydrates 65.1g
Protein 18.1 g
Cholesterol 35 mg
Sodium 789 mg

Ingredients

1 (12 oz) package dried rice noodles
1 tsp vegetable oil
1 onion, finely diced
3 cloves garlic, minced
2 C. diced cooked chicken breast meat
1 small head cabbage, thinly sliced
4 carrot, thinly sliced
1/4 C. soy sauce
2 lemons - cut into wedges, for garnish

Directions

1. Get a large bowl: Fill it with hot water. Place it in the noodles and place it aside until it becomes soft.
2. Place a large pan over medium heat. Heat the oil in it. Add the garlic with onion and cook them for 3 min.
3. Stir in the carrot with chicken and cabbage. Cook them for 6 min. Stir in the noodles and cook them for 3 min while stirring constantly. Serve your chicken stir fry hot.
4. Enjoy.

Sweet and Salty Chicken Stir Fry

Prep Time: 20 mins
Total Time: 40 mins

Servings per Recipe: 4
Calories	615 kcal
Fat	33.2 g
Carbohydrates	37.9 g
Protein	43 g
Cholesterol	129 mg
Sodium	1967 mg

Ingredients

- 3/4 C. dark brown sugar
- 1/3 C. cold water
- 1/3 C. fish sauce
- 1/3 C. rice vinegar
- 1 tbsp soy sauce
- 4 cloves garlic, crushed
- 1 tbsp fresh grated ginger
- 1 tsp vegetable oil
- 8 boneless, skinless chicken thighs, quartered
- 1/2 C. roasted peanuts
- 2 fresh jalapeno peppers, seeded and sliced
- 1 bunch green onions, chopped
- fresh cilantro sprigs, for garnish

Directions

1. Get a medium mixing bowl: Combine in it the brown sugar, water, fish sauce, rice vinegar, soy sauce, garlic, and ginger. Mix them well to make the sauce and place it aside for 2 min.
2. Place a large pan over medium heat. Heat the oil in it. Cook in it the chicken with 1/3 C. of the sauce for 8 min.
3. Stir in the remaining sauce and cook them for 7 min. Add the peanuts, jalapenos and green onion. Cook them for 4 min.
4. Serve your chicken stir fry hot with some rice.
5. Enjoy.

CHILI FRIED Chicken Breast Bites

Prep Time: 30 mins
Total Time: 50 mins

Servings per Recipe: 4
Calories   740 kcal
Fat   37 g
Carbohydrates 68.3g
Protein   34 g
Cholesterol   86 mg
Sodium   1113 mg

Ingredients

2 tbsp soy sauce
1 tbsp apple cider
1 dash sesame oil
2 tbsp all-purpose flour
2 tbsp cornstarch
2 tbsp water
1/4 tsp baking powder
1/4 tsp baking soda
1 tsp canola oil
4 (5 oz) skinless, boneless chicken breast halves, cut into 1-inch cubes
1 quart vegetable oil for frying
1/2 C. water
1 C. chicken broth
1/4 C. distilled white vinegar
1/4 C. cornstarch
1 C. white sugar
2 tbsp soy sauce
2 tbsp sesame oil
1 tsp red chile paste (such as Thai Kitchen(R))
1 clove garlic, minced
2 tbsp toasted sesame seeds

Directions

1. Get a large mixing bowl: Mix in it the 2 tbsp soy sauce, apple cider, dash of sesame oil, flour, 2 tbsp cornstarch, 2 tbsp water, baking powder, baking soda, and canola oil.
2. Add the chicken and stir them. Place a plastic wrap over the bowl. Place it in the fridge for 30 min.
3. Heat the oil in a heavy saucepan until it reaches 375 F.
4. Place a heavy saucepan over medium heat: Stir in it 1/2 C. water, chicken broth, vinegar, 1/4 C. cornstarch, sugar, 2 tbsp soy sauce, 2 tbsp sesame oil, red chili paste, and garlic .
5. Cook them until they start boiling while stirring all the time to make the sauce. Lower the heat and keep cooking the sauce until it becomes slightly thick.
6. Drain the chicken from the marinade and deep fry it for 4 to 6 min or until it becomes golden brown.
7. Remove the chicken dices from the hot oil and serve them with the sauce warm.
8. Enjoy.

Made in the USA
Columbia, SC
08 November 2022